Circle - Circum = πD

Area = πR² = ¼ πD²

area ☑ **W9-BJA-169**

BASIC FLUID MECHANICS

BASIC FLUID MECHANICS

McGRAW-HILL BOOK COMPANY, INC.

NEW YORK

TORONTO

LONDON

by J. LISTER ROBINSON

LECTURER IN MECHANICAL

ENGINEERING AT

THE EASTERN ONTARIO INSTITUTE

OF TECHNOLOGY

BASIC FLUID MECHANICS

TO MAUREEN

TO MAUGHAM

Preface

The subject of fluid mechanics is a vast and complex one that deals with the behavior of all types of fluid either at rest or in motion. Since a great deal of fluid behavior is impossible or extremely complex to analyze mathematically, it is often necessary to resort to experimental data to obtain working results. This tends to make the study of fluid mechanics rather overwhelming for the student meeting it for the first time; and therefore it is essential to use a simple and straightforward approach in an elementary fluid mechanics course.

This text is intended to meet the need of students attending technical institutes and colleges. It deals with the subject at a level which will be easily comprehensible to them, at the same time giving them sufficient knowledge to deal with the practical fluid mechanics problems that they are likely to encounter in their later work.

Throughout this book the mathematics have been kept as simple as possible, and the work may be covered coincidently with a first course in calculus. The work content of the book is about 150 classroom hours for technological students, although it may be completed more rapidly by advanced students using it as an introduction to an advanced fluid mechanics course.

At the end of each chapter are a number of problems for the student to solve. If each problem is properly completed and understood by the student, all the principles involved will be clear to him.

Reference to experimental data has been kept to a minimum since it is assumed that the student will receive experimental instruction in a parallel laboratory course.

J. L. Robinson

Contents

ix

CHAPTER 1

The Properties of a Fluid

1·1 The definition of a fluid

A fluid may be defined as a substance which is incapable of resisting shearing forces when in static equilibrium. To illustrate this, consider the riveted joint shown in Fig. 1·1. The rivet is subject to a pure shear force across the face AB and will hold until the applied shear force is sufficient to cause the metal to fail. It is obvious that if the rivet were replaced with a fluid, then the smallest applied force would be sufficient to cause distortion. The reason for this is the complete inability of the fluid to resist a static shearing force.

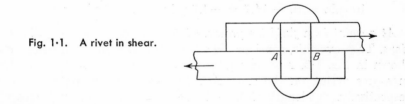

Fig. 1·1.   A rivet in shear.

The inability of a fluid to resist a shear force is caused by the large molecular spacing within fluids. In a solid the molecules are closely packed and the intermolecular forces are large, enabling a solid to resist any change of shape. However, liquid molecular spacing is much greater with correspondingly smaller cohesive forces, enabling the molecules to move more freely. This gives a liquid the ability to flow.

A division of fluids into two categories, liquids and gases, is possible because of the extremely large molecular gap which occurs in gases. These very large gaps cause gases to flow more easily than liquids and give gases their extreme compressibility.

Since at a solid-fluid boundary there can be no shear stress within a static fluid, it follows that any force exerted by the fluid on the solid must act normally to the surface, whatever the shape of the surface may be, so that the tangential or shearing component of the force is zero.

Although fluids consist of discrete molecules, the study of fluid mechanics treats fluids as continuous media, which is justifiable since the molecular size and movement are infinitesimal in comparison with the distances involved in engineering applications.

1·2   Fluid pressure

The pressure of a fluid is measured in terms of force per unit area, usually pounds per square inch (psi) or pounds per square foot (psf). Since at ground level the weight of the atmosphere is sufficient to produce an atmospheric pressure of 14.7 psi, it is usual to designate pressures as gage or absolute to indicate whether they are relative to atmospheric or zero pressure. *A gage pressure is the difference between the pressure being measured and the surrounding atmospheric pressure,* whereas *an absolute pressure is the sum of the gage pressure and the atmospheric pressure.* In order to differentiate between them, these pressures are written as psig and psia.

Example:

$$5 \text{ psig} = 14.7 + 5 = 19.7 \text{ psia}$$
$$10 \text{ psia} = 10 - 14.7 = -4.7 \text{ psig} = 4.7 \text{ psi of vacuum}$$

At a point in a fluid the pressure intensity acts equally in all directions. To prove this, consider the small fluid element of unit thickness shown in Fig. 1·2. ABC is a right-angled triangle with $AB = a$. The pressures acting on the sides AC, BC, and AB are p_1, p_2, and p_3 respectively. The length of these sides are $a \cos \theta$, $a \sin \theta$, and a respectively. Therefore the forces acting on these three sides are $p_1 a \cos \theta$, $p_2 a \sin \theta$, and $p_3 a$ in that order.

Resolving these forces horizontally and vertically for equilibrium conditions gives

$$p_3 a \sin \theta = p_2 a \sin \theta$$
$$p_3 a \cos \theta = p_1 a \cos \theta$$

Therefore $$p_1 = p_2 = p_3$$

In Fig. 1·3 the small surface area A is acted on by a pressure p normal to the surface, since no shear can exist. The force acting on this surface is pA, and the horizontal component is $pA \cos \theta$. But $A \cos \theta = S$, the vertical projection of the area A. *Hence it follows that*

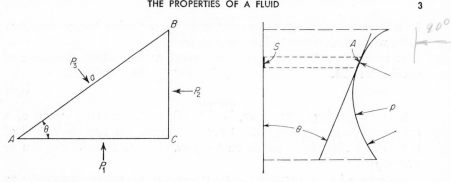

Fig. 1·2. Pressure forces acting on an element of fluid.

Fig. 1·3. Pressure force acting on a curved area.

the total horizontal force on the entire surface is given by the product of the pressure and the vertically projected area.

Example: The end plate of a boiler consists of a hemispherical cap of 5-ft diameter, as shown in Fig. 1·4. The boiler contains steam at a

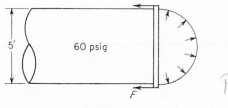

Fig. 1·4

pressure of 60 psig. What is the force required to hold the cap in position?

Total end thrust = pressure × projected area of cap
$$= \frac{60 \times 144 \times 25\pi}{4} \text{ lb}$$
$$= 84.8 \text{ short tons}$$

1·3 Specific weight, density, specific gravity, and specific volume

Specific weight is defined as weight per unit volume and has the symbol γ (gamma). The units of specific weight are pounds per cubic foot (lb/ft³).

Density is defined as mass per unit volume and is given the symbol ρ (rho). The units of density are slugs per cubic foot (slugs/ft³). The slug unit has been introduced by engineers to avoid confusion between weight and mass. One slug of mass actually weighs g pounds. It will be seen later that the use of the slug often avoids the necessity of dividing by g in order to keep units consistent.

It is now possible to write an equation connecting density and specific weight.

$$\gamma = \rho g \tag{1.1}$$

Specific gravity, S or sp gr, is the ratio of the specific weight of a substance to the specific weight of pure water. The specific weight of pure water actually depends on temperature but is usually taken as 62.4 lb/ft³.

Because of this variation with temperature and the necessity to quote temperatures when using specific gravities, it is more usual to use density or specific weight when dealing with fluids encountered in engineering problems.

Specific volume V is the reciprocal of specific weight and thus has units of cubic feet per pound (ft³/lb).

$$V = \frac{1}{\gamma} \tag{1.2}$$

1.4 Viscosity

Although fluids offer no resistance to shear when in equilibrium, some flow much more easily than others. Heavy oil, for instance, flows very sluggishly in comparison with water. The unit with which this sluggishness is measured is called viscosity, the thickest fluids being the most viscous.

The cause of viscosity is the molecular cohesion and interaction between adjacent layers of fluid. When a fluid is at rest, there is no resistance to an applied shear force, which will cause the fluid to commence to flow. As soon as this flow is started, a resistance is encountered which varies with the viscosity of the fluid, and shearing forces are established.

Consider a fluid flowing over a smooth surface so that any fluid particle has motion parallel to the surface only (see Fig. 1.5). Such a flow is called laminar because the fluid moves in layers or "laminae."

Next to the surface, molecules of the fluid become embedded in the solid wall, and this layer of fluid is obviously at rest relative to the wall. Further from the wall the fluid has velocity v, which increases with distance from the wall y, giving a velocity distribution as shown in Fig. 1.5.

Now consider two adjacent layers of fluid having velocities v and $v + dv$ respectively and distance dy apart. The layer most remote from the wall has a velocity dv relative to the adjacent layer, and this causes a viscous or shearing stress to be present between the two layers. This stress is given the symbol τ (tau). The coefficient of viscosity μ (mu) is defined as the ratio

$$\frac{\text{Shearing stress}}{\text{Rate of shearing strain}}$$

and may be compared with the modulus of rigidity of a solid.

The rate of shearing strain is given by dv/dy, and hence

$$\mu = \frac{\tau}{dv/dy}$$

or
$$\tau = \mu \frac{dv}{dy} \qquad (1\cdot3)$$

μ is also called the absolute or dynamic viscosity and has units of lb-sec/ft² or slugs/ft-sec.

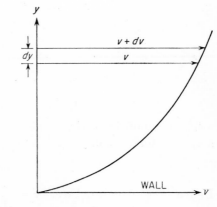

Fig. 1·5. Laminar flow profile close to a boundary.

A distinct difference exists between fluids of liquid and gaseous natures in the effect of temperature on the value of their dynamic viscosity. Increase of temperature causes a decrease in the viscosity of a liquid and an increase in the viscosity of a gas, with a few rare exceptions.

Referring back to Fig. 1·5, at the surface the shear stress is supported by the wall itself and appears as friction drag on the wall. Equation (1·3) makes it possible to estimate this friction drag from the relationship

$$\tau_{\text{wall}} = \mu \frac{dv}{dy}_{\text{wall}} \qquad (1\cdot4)$$

Example 1: A block weighing 100 lb and having an area of 2 ft² slides down an inclined plane as shown in Fig. 1·6, with a constant velocity. An oil gap between the block and the plane is 0.01 in. thick, the inclination of the plane is 30° to the horizontal, and the velocity of the block is 6 fps. Find the viscosity of the lubricating film.

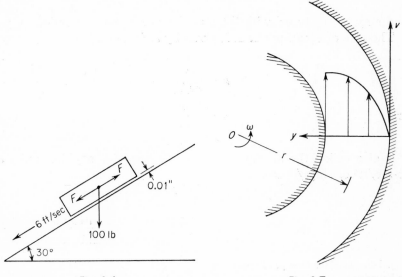

Fig. 1·6   Fig. 1·7

The component of the weight acting down the plane is opposed by a viscous force exactly equal and opposite to it. Therefore

$$F = 100 \sin 30° = 50 \text{ lb}$$

Hence

$$\tau = \frac{F}{A} = \frac{50}{2} = 25 \text{ psf}$$

but

$$\tau = \mu \frac{dv}{dy}$$

Therefore

$$\int_0^{\frac{0.01}{12}} 25 \, dy = \mu \int_0^6 dv$$

i.e.,

$$6\mu = \frac{25 \times 0.01}{12}$$

 $\mu = 0.00347 \text{ lb-sec/ft}^2$

Example 2: A shaft 4 in. in diameter revolves at 3,000 rpm in a bearing with a clearance of 0.01 in. all round. The gap is filled with oil of viscosity 120×10^{-5} lb-sec/ft². Find the torque lost per foot of bearing.

Consider 1 ft of the bearing. dv/dy can be written as $-dv/dr$, since $y = -r$ (see Fig. 1·7). Now at a radius of r feet the torque can be written as

$$T = \tau \times \text{surface area} \times r$$

$$= \mu \times -\frac{dv}{dr} \times 2\pi r \times r$$

$$= -2\mu\pi r^2 \frac{dv}{dr}$$

$$= \text{a constant across the gap}$$

Therefore
$$\frac{dv}{dr} = -\frac{T}{2\mu\pi r^2}$$

Hence, by integrating,

$$v = -\frac{T}{2\pi\mu} \int \frac{dr}{r^2} = -\frac{T}{2\pi\mu}\left(c - \frac{1}{r}\right)$$

where c is a constant of integration.

Now when $r = \frac{2}{12}$ ft, $v = \omega r = 3{,}000 \times 2\pi \times 2/60 \times 12 = 52.4$ fps and when $r = 2.01/12$ ft, $v = 0$ (since at the surface there is no relative velocity between the fluid and the wall). Hence

$$c = \frac{12}{2.01}$$

which gives

$$T = \frac{2\pi\mu v}{1/r - c} = 13.25 \text{ lb-ft/ft}$$

The student should show that for a sufficiently small gap, as in this problem, dv/dy can be closely approximated to v/y.

The ratio μ/ρ occurs frequently in the study of fluid mechanics and is termed the kinematic viscosity ν (nu). The units of kinematic viscosity are square feet per second (ft²/sec) or square centimeters per second (cm²/sec). One cm²/sec is called a stoke, after Sir George Stokes, and since this is rather a large unit, it is more usual to deal with 0.01 stoke, which is called a centistoke. In this text, however, only engineering units of ft²/sec will be used.

1·5 Surface tension

When two immiscible fluids, such as air and water, are in contact with one another, a slight pressure difference is observed across the contact surface. The pressure is supported by the contact surface which acts as though it were an elastic skin, stretched and in tension in every direction. This tension force is called surface tension σ (sigma) and has units of force per unit length, usually pounds per foot (lb/ft).

If a needle is placed on a piece of blotting paper and the blotting paper then floated on the surface of a bowl of water, the blotting paper will eventually sink and leave the needle "floating" on the water, supported by the surface tension effect.

A soap bubble is maintained by the surface tension of the film. Consider half a bubble as shown in Fig. 1·8. The two halves of the

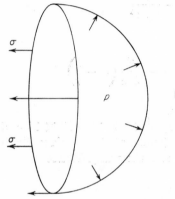

Fig. 1·8.　Surface tension forces.

bubble are, of course, in equilibrium. The excess pressure inside the bubble is p, and the total force acting to the right is

$$p \times \text{projected area of the bubble} = p \times \frac{\pi d^2}{4}$$

The force resisting this is supplied by the surface tension and has magnitude

$$\pi\, d\, \sigma$$

Therefore
$$\pi\, d\, \sigma = p \times \frac{\pi d^2}{4}$$

or
$$p = \frac{4\sigma}{d} \tag{1·5}$$

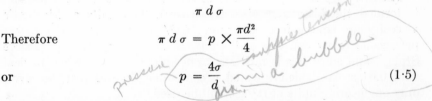

Equation (1·5) gives the relationship between the pressure in a bubble and its diameter. It will be observed that the pressure decreases with an increase in diameter. This can readily be verified by using the apparatus shown in Fig. 1·9. Two bubbles of different size are blown at A and B and isolated by closing taps D and E. When tap C is closed and the two bubbles are connected by opening D and E, the small bubble will deflate and thus inflate the larger one.

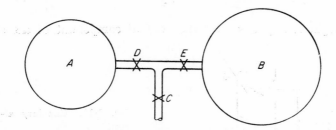
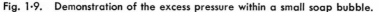

Fig. 1·9. Demonstration of the excess pressure within a small soap bubble.

1·6 Contact angle and capillarity

When a liquid comes into contact with a solid, the surface tension effect causes the surface of the liquid close to the boundary to rise or fall, according to the conditions that prevail, to form a curved surface or meniscus. Figure 1·10 shows water and mercury in contact with a glass surface. The angle made between the liquid surface and the solid boundary is called the contact angle. Combinations with an upward-curving meniscus, such as in Fig. 1·10a, have contact angles

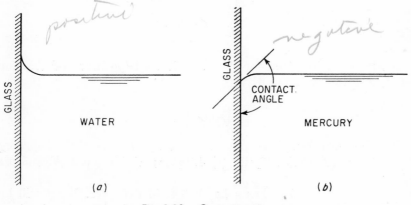

Fig. 1·10. Contact angle.

between 0 and 90°; those with a downward-curving meniscus have contact angles between 90 and 180°. This meniscus effect causes a liquid to rise or fall in an open tube placed in a liquid, which is called capillarity or the capillary effect.

Neglecting the amount of liquid above the bottom of the meniscus in Fig. 1·11, the weight of liquid in the tube above the general surface level is

$$h\gamma \frac{\pi d^2}{4}$$

This weight is supported by the vertical component of the surface

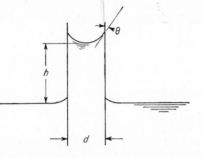

Fig. 1·11. Capillary effect.

tension at the edge of the meniscus. If θ is the contact angle, the vertical component is

$$\pi d \sigma \cos \theta$$

Equating these,

$$h\gamma \frac{\pi d^2}{4} = \pi d \sigma \cos \theta$$

Hence

$$h = \frac{4\sigma \cos \theta}{\gamma d}$$

It will be noticed that for $0° \leqslant \theta < 90°$, h is positive and that for $90° \leqslant \theta < 180°$, h is negative.

PROBLEMS

1·1   Taking atmospheric pressure as 14.7 psia, convert the following pressures to psig: (a) 16 psia; (b) 4.2 psia; (c) 965 psfa; (d) 605 psf of vacuum.

1·2   A diving sphere has a hatch 3 ft in diameter. What will be the force on the hatch when the sphere is submerged to a depth where the water pressure is 100 psig?

1·3   A living dome to be erected on the moon consists of part of a sphere having a diameter of 30 ft at the base and a maximum height of 10 ft. If the pressure within the dome is 9 psia (outside pressure is zero), calculate the force tending to lift the dome.

1·4   A pipe 6 in. in diameter is welded along the seam. What is the force per inch along the weld when the pipe contains a fluid under 30 psig pressure?

1·5 An automobile hydraulic brake system has a master brake cylinder 2 in. in diameter. The individual cylinders on each wheel are $\frac{3}{4}$ in. in diameter. What force is exerted at each wheel for a brake pedal force of 100 lb? (Assume that the brake pedal force is applied directly to the master cylinder.) If each wheel piston (eight in all) moves a total distance of $\frac{1}{4}$ in., calculate the required movement of the master cylinder piston.

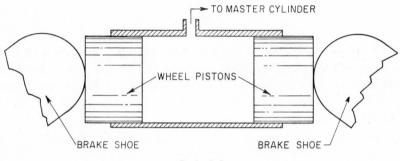

Prob. 1·5

1·6 An automobile hydraulic lift has a ram diameter of 1 ft. What supply pressure is required to lift a combined car and ram weight of 3,000 lb? If a pump is available with an output of 0.2 cfs at the required pressure, how long will it take to lift the car 6 ft?

1·7 The density of air at standard atmospheric conditions is 0.00238 slugs/ft³. What is the weight of 17 ft³ of such air?

1·8 A block of wood weighing 30 lb slides at a constant speed down an inclined plane. The angle of inclination is 45°, the contact area of the wood is 1.5 ft², and the velocity is 10 fps. If the wood slides on an oil film with $\mu = 0.007$ lb-sec/ft², find the thickness of the oil film.

1·9 A flat plate of area 0.5 ft² moves in oil parallel to and midway between two large flat plates, 12 in. apart with a velocity of 10 fps. If the viscosity of the oil is 6×10^{-5} lb-sec/ft², calculate the drag on the plate.

1·10 If the plate of the previous problem moves 3 in. from one large plate and 9 in. from the other, what will be the drag?

1·11 A ground-effect vehicle rides on a cushion of air 3 in. thick. If the diameter of the base of the machine is 16 ft, calculate the viscous resistance due to the air cushion at 50 mph.

1·12 A shaft 6 in. in diameter and revolving at 3,000 rpm is supported in a bearing 6 in. long. If the gap between the shaft and the bearing surface is 0.01 in. around the shaft and contains a lubricant of $\mu = 105 \times 10^{-5}$ lb-sec/ft², find the horsepower loss due to the friction.

1·13 A torque of 0.3 lb-in. is required to turn a cylinder 1 ft long and 2 in. in diameter concentrically within a fixed cylinder of 2.2-in. inside diameter at a rate of 6 rad/sec. Determine the coefficient of viscosity of the fluid between the two cylinders.

1·14 Show that the pressure and diameter of a spherical bubble immersed in water are related by the expression

$$p = \frac{4\sigma}{d}$$

1·15 If an open glass tube of 0.05-in. bore is placed in a dish of mercury, will the capillary effect cause the level in the tube to be above or below the free surface, and by how much? (For mercury take $\gamma = 850$ lb/ft³, $\sigma = 0.035$ lb/ft, and the contact angle for glass-mercury = 130°.)

CHAPTER 2

Fluid Statics

The subject of fluid mechanics is divided into three subgroups: fluid statics, hydrodynamics, and gas dynamics. The study of fluid statics is the simplest of these three groups, because it deals only with fluids at rest, in which state viscosity does not enter into the analysis.

2·1 The pressure-density-height relationship

Consider the container shown in Fig. 2·1. A column of liquid of specific weight γ and height h is supported in the container by the base, which has an area A. The weight of the liquid contained is $\gamma A h$, and

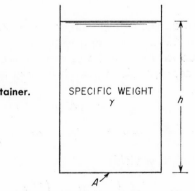

Fig. 2·1. A fluid container.

SPECIFIC WEIGHT
γ

h

A

the area supporting this weight is A. The pressure of the liquid on the base, then, is

$$p = \frac{\gamma A h}{A} = \gamma h \qquad (2·1)$$

13

This is dependent only upon the specific weight of the fluid and the height of the fluid. Thus it is possible to express a pressure as a "head" of liquid, for example, feet of water or inches of mercury.

If the column of liquid is replaced by a compressible fluid, that is to say, a gas, then the derivation of the pressure at the base of the column is a little more complex. Consider a small element of a column of gas as shown in Fig. 2·2. A is the cross-sectional area of the column and hence the area of the element; γ is the specific weight of the gas at this point. (It must be noted that γ is now a variable.) For the element to be

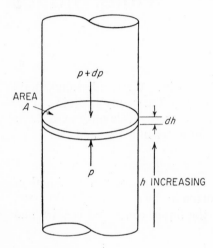

Fig. 2·2. A small element of fluid in equilibrium.

in equilibrium, the sum of the downward forces on the element must be equal to the sum of the upward forces.

Acting downward are the pressure force $(p + dp)A$ and the weight of the element $\gamma A \, dh$. Supporting these is the upward pressure force pA. Hence

$$pA = \gamma A \, dh + (p + dp)A$$

Therefore $-\gamma \, dh = dp$ or $\dfrac{dp}{dh} = -\gamma$

Integrating this yields

$$-\int_{h_1}^{h_2} \gamma \, dh = \int_{p_1}^{p_2} dp = p_2 - p_1 \qquad (2\cdot2)$$

If γ is regarded as a constant in Eq. 2·2, the equation reduces to

$$\gamma(h_1 - h_2) = (p_2 - p_1)$$

Considering the pressure at the bottom of a column of height h, so that

$p_1 = p$, $p_2 = 0$, $h_1 = 0$, and $h_2 = h$, this reduces to

$$\gamma h = p$$

which agrees with Eq. (2·1).

Example: A column of compressible fluid of height h_1 has a specific weight which varies linearly from 0 at the top of the column to γ_1 at the base, as shown in Fig. 2·3. Show that the difference in pressures at the top and bottom of the column is the same as that for a similar column of constant specific weight equal to $\gamma_1/2$.

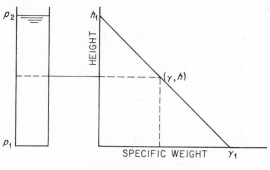

Fig. 2·3

The pressure difference for a fluid of constant specific weight $\gamma_1/2$ is

$$p_1 - p_2 = \frac{h_1\gamma_1}{2}$$

For the compressible fluid

$$p_1 - p_2 = \int_0^{h_1} \gamma\, dh$$

But

$$\frac{\gamma_1}{h_1} = \frac{\gamma}{h_1 - h}$$

therefore

$$\gamma = \frac{\gamma_1(h_1 - h)}{h_1}$$

Hence

$$p_1 - p_2 = \int_0^{h_1} \frac{\gamma_1(h_1 - h)\, dh}{h_1}$$

$$= \frac{\gamma_1}{h_1} \int_0^{h_1} (h_1 - h)\, dh$$

$$= \frac{\gamma_1}{h_1}\left[h_1 h - \frac{h^2}{2} \right]_0^{h_1} = \frac{\gamma_1 h_1}{2} \qquad \text{QED}$$

2·2   Manometers

Since a pressure can be expressed in terms of a head of liquid, it is possible to measure pressures with a liquid head device. A manometer is an instrument that uses this principle. Figure 2·4 shows a simple manometer which consists of a U-tube of glass AB, containing a liquid of known specific weight. One end of the tube is open to atmosphere, and the other end is connected to the pressure source to be measured. The excess pressure in the arm B, that is to say, the gage pressure in B, causes the liquid to move in the tube until equilibrium is reached. At

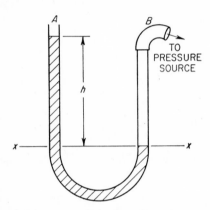

Fig. 2·4.   A simple manometer.

this point the pressures in both arms at the datum level x-x are equal. Hence the *gage* pressure being measured is given by

$$p = \gamma h$$

Example: One arm of a simple U-tube manometer containing mercury is connected to a pressure source, and the other arm is open to the atmosphere (14.7 psi). The mercury in the open arm is seen to be 17.55 in. above the level in the other arm. What is the pressure being measured in psia? (γ for mercury is 850 lb/ft³.)

$$h = 17.55 \text{ in.} = \frac{17.55}{12} \text{ ft}$$

$$p = \gamma h = \frac{850 \times 17.55}{12} \text{ psfg}$$

$$= \frac{850 \times 17.55}{12 \times 144} \text{ psig}$$

$$= 8.95 + 14.7 \text{ psia}$$

$$= 23.65 \text{ psia}$$

2·3 Pressure measurement and variations of the simple manometer

The range of pressure measurements made in fluid mechanics extends from hundreds of pounds per square inch to fractions of a pound per square foot. In order to cover such a large range, many types of pressure gages are used.

The Bourdon gage. This type of gage consists of a tube bent into a circular form and sealed at one end, as shown in Fig. 2·5. When a pressure is applied at the open end, the tube tends to straighten out and actuates a linkage which causes a needle to move over a calibrated scale.

Fig. 2·5. The Bourdon gage.

gage pressure.

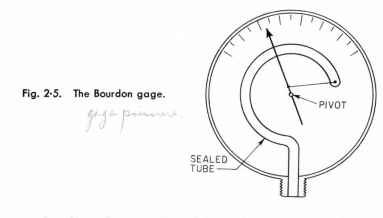

PIVOT

SEALED
TUBE

A properly adjusted gage will read zero when disconnected, so it will be seen that such an instrument reads gage pressures, to which the local atmospheric pressure must be added if absolute pressures are required.

Vacuum pressures may also be read with Bourdon gages since a pressure lower than atmospheric within the tube will cause it to contract and thus move the needle in the opposite direction.

Bourdon gages are made in a great variety of sensitivities and may be used to measure high or low pressures accordingly.

The pressure transducer. The pressure transducer consists basically of a small strain gage attached to a diaphragm. The diaphragm is mounted in a short tube, and the space behind the diaphragm is evacuated (Fig. 2·6). Application of pressure causes the diaphragm to deflect and thus changes the electrical resistance of the strain gage. This change in resistance is measured electrically and converted into pressure from the transducer calibration.

The transducer has the advantage that it will read absolute pressures directly, independent of the ambient atmospheric pressure, if the space behind the diaphragm is evacuated. If this space is open to the atmosphere, then, of course, the instrument will read gage pressures.

Transducers are also made in a variety of sensitivities and may be used for any pressure range. One great advantage is that they are usually small and easily fitted in places that might otherwise be inaccessible.

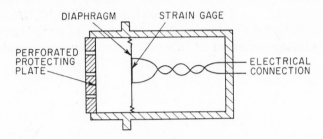

Fig. 2·6.   A pressure transducer.

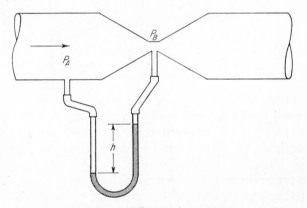

Fig. 2·7.   A differential manometer.

The differential manometer. The differential manometer is used to measure pressure differences. It differs from the simple manometer only in that each end of the U-tube is connected to a pressure source, and the difference in levels of the liquid in the two arms gives the difference between the two pressure sources being measured. Thus, for Fig. 2·7,

$$p_A - p_B = h(\gamma_G - \gamma_F)$$

where γ_G = specific weight of gage fluid
      γ_F = specific weight of fluid flowing

The inclined manometer. By inclining a simple manometer at an angle θ to the vertical, it can be made more sensitive. A vertical head of h (Fig. 2·8) will produce a larger inclined head of $h \sec \theta$ when so inclined; and since $\sec \theta$ varies from 1 to infinity as θ varies from 0 to 90°, it is apparent that the larger θ becomes, the more sensitive the manometer becomes. A practical limit is reached, however, when the meniscus of the liquid in the tube becomes very large and offsets the gain in sensitivity.

Inclined manometers are usually arranged on a board which may be rotated through any desired angle. The pressure can then be calculated by using the relationship

$$p = \gamma h' \cos \theta \qquad (2\cdot3)$$

where $h' = $ measured inclined head
$\qquad \theta = $ angle of inclination from the vertical

Fig. 2·8.   An inclined manometer.

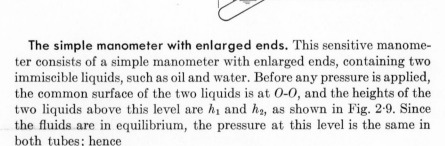

The simple manometer with enlarged ends. This sensitive manometer consists of a simple manometer with enlarged ends, containing two immiscible liquids, such as oil and water. Before any pressure is applied, the common surface of the two liquids is at O-O, and the heights of the two liquids above this level are h_1 and h_2, as shown in Fig. 2·9. Since the fluids are in equilibrium, the pressure at this level is the same in both tubes; hence

$$h_1\gamma_1 = h_2\gamma_2 \qquad (2\cdot4)$$

where γ_1 and γ_2 are the specific weights of the two fluids. A pressure is applied to one arm of the tube, which causes the fluids to be displaced, and the common surface descends an amount y to the new datum O'-O'. The levels of the two liquids above the common surface are now x_1 and x_2, and the applied pressure p is given by

$$x_1\gamma_1 = x_2\gamma_2 + p$$
or
$$p = x_1\gamma_1 - x_2\gamma_2 \qquad (2\cdot5)$$

But if the common surface descended an amount y, the open surface in

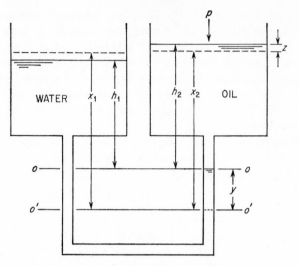

Fig. 2·9.   An enlarged-ended U-tube manometer.

the enlarged ends must have descended or risen by an amount z, so that

$$Az = ay \qquad (2·6)$$

where A = area of cross section of large ends
a = area of cross section of tube

Also $x_1 = h_1 + z + y$
and $x_2 = h_2 - z + y$

Substituting these in Eq. (2.5) gives

$$p = \gamma_1(h_1 + z + y) - \gamma_2(h_2 - z + y)$$
$$= \gamma_1(z + y) - \gamma_2(y - z)$$

since $\gamma_1 h_1 = \gamma_2 h_2$. Now

$$z = \frac{a}{A} y$$

Therefore $p = y\left[\gamma_1\left(1 + \frac{a}{A}\right) - \gamma_2\left(1 - \frac{a}{A}\right)\right] \qquad (2·7)$

Example: An enlarged-ended U-tube manometer contains water in one limb ($\gamma = 62.4$ lb/ft³) and oil in the other ($\gamma = 48.0$ lb/ft³). The diameter of the large ends is 1 in., and the bore of the tube is 0.197 in.

Application of pressure to the side containing oil causes a movement of the common surface of 3 in. What is the applied pressure?

$$p = y\left[\gamma_1\left(1 + \frac{a}{A}\right) - \gamma_2\left(1 - \frac{a}{A}\right)\right]$$

$$\frac{a}{A} = 0.197^2 = 0.0387$$

Therefore $p = \frac{3}{12}(62.4 \times 1.0387 - 48.0 \times 0.9613)$
$$= 4.67 \text{ psf}$$
$$= 0.0324 \text{ psig}$$

2·4 Pressure forces on submerged plane surfaces

When a body is immersed in a fluid, the fluid exerts a pressure normal to the surface at all points where the body and fluid come into contact. Thus, a piece of paper held in the atmosphere has a pressure of 14.7 psi acting over its entire surface. The force is not felt, however, since the total force on each side of the paper is the same, resulting in a net force of zero. However, if the atmosphere came into contact with one side only, then a considerable force would be exerted. This can be demonstrated by placing a sheet of newspaper on a flat table so that the edge of the paper reaches the edge of the table and by placing a thin wooden ruler underneath the paper with a few inches projecting over the table edge. A sharp blow on the ruler will cause it to snap without disturbing the paper, owing to the very large atmospheric force on the paper.

Pressure forces can be very great when dealing with liquids, and the calculation of such forces is important in designing dams, weirs, lock gates, bulkheads, and many other structures.

The pressure forces exerted by gases (or by liquids acting on entirely horizontal surfaces) are easy to calculate simply by multiplying the pressure by the surface area. When dealing with nonhorizontal surfaces immersed in liquids, it is necessary to consider the pressure variation across the surface.

The pressure intensity at the horizontal strip (Fig. 2·10) is γh. Hence the force on this strip is

$$\Delta F = \gamma h \, dA$$

and the total force on the whole area is given by

$$F = \int_A^B \gamma h \, dA$$
$$= \gamma \int_A^B h \, dA$$

But $h\,dA$ equals the moment of area of the small strip about a line drawn in the surface, and so

$$\int_A^B h\,dA = Ah_c \qquad \text{total moment of area}$$

where h_c = vertical distance from centroid of area to surface
      A = total area

So the total force on a plane submerged surface is given by

$$F = \gamma Ah_c \tag{2·8}$$

which is to say that *the force is equal to the product of the area and the*

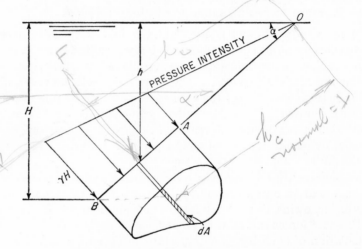

Fig. 2·10.   An immersed flat plate.

pressure at the centroid of the area. This force acts normally to the surface so that, if the surface is inclined at an angle α to the horizontal, the horizontal component is given by

$$F_H = F \sin \alpha$$

Example 1: A sluice gate extends from 5 to 10 ft below the surface of the water, as shown in Fig. 2·11. Calculate the force on the gate if the gate is 4 ft wide.

At a depth h the pressure intensity is γh. Therefore the force on a small horizontal strip at this depth is given by

$$\Delta F = \gamma h 4\,dh$$

and hence

$$F = \int_5^{10} 4\gamma h\,dh = 9{,}360 \text{ lb}$$

Or alternatively

> Depth of centroid of the area = 7.5 ft
> Pressure at this depth = 7.5 × 62.4 psf

Thus the total force on the gate is

$$7.5 \times 62.4 \times 5 \times 4 = 9{,}360 \text{ lb}$$

Example 2: A dam 4,000 ft long contains water 100 ft deep. The face

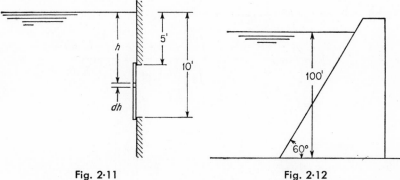

Fig. 2·11   Fig. 2·12

of the dam slopes at 60° to the horizontal, as shown in Fig. 2.12. What is the total horizontal force on the dam?

> Depth of centroid = 50 ft
> Pressure at centroid = 50 × 62.4 psf

Therefore the total force acting on the dam horizontally is

$$50 \times 62.4 \times \text{projected vertical area} = 50 \times 62.4 \times 100 \times 4{,}000$$
$$= 1.25 \times 10^9 \text{ lb}$$

2·5 Center of pressure

Having established the total pressure force acting on a submerged area, it can be considered a single force acting at a point called the *center of pressure*, at a depth $\bar{h}$.

Referring back to Fig. 2·10 and taking moments about O,

$$F\bar{h} \operatorname{cosec} \alpha = \sum \Delta F\, h \operatorname{cosec} \alpha = \int_A^B h\, dA\, h \operatorname{cosec} \alpha$$

or

$$\bar{h} = \frac{\int_A^B \gamma h^2\, dA}{F} = \frac{\int_A^B \gamma h^2\, dA}{\int_A^B \gamma h\, dA} \qquad (2\cdot9)$$

Example: Find the position of the center of pressure of the sluice gate in Example 1 of Art. 2·4 (see Fig. 2·13).

The force acting on the small horizontal strip is

$$\gamma h 4\ dh$$

and the moment of this about the surface is

$$\gamma h^2 4\ dh$$

If $\bar{h}$ is the depth of the center of pressure, then

$$F\bar{h} = \int_5^{10} \gamma h^2 4\ dh$$

or

$$\bar{h} = \frac{\int_5^{10} \gamma h^2 4\ dh}{F} = \frac{\int_5^{10} \gamma h^2 4\ dh}{\int_5^{10} \gamma h 4\ dh} = \frac{\int_5^{10} h^2\ dh}{\int_5^{10} h\ dh}$$

$$= \frac{[h^3/3]_5^{10}}{[h^2/2]_5^{10}} = 7.78 \text{ ft}$$

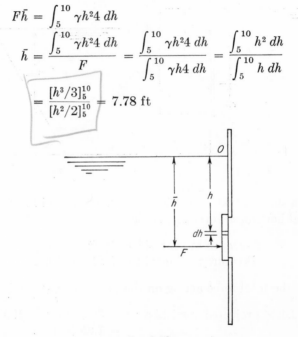

Fig. 2·13

Center of pressure by moments of inertia method. In the preceding article the vertical depth of the center of pressure of a plane area was established as

$$\bar{h} = \frac{\int_A^B h^2\ dA}{\int_A^B h\ dA} \qquad (2\cdot9)$$

Now $\int_A^B h^2\ dA$ is the second moment of area, or the moment of inertia, of the area concerned about the surface, or I_{surf}. The quantity $\int_A^B h\ dA$

is the first moment of area about the surface, or Ah_c. Thus

$$\bar{h} = \frac{I_{\text{surf}}}{Ah_c}$$

Moments of inertia are usually quoted about an axis passing through the centroid; shifting the axis from the surface to a *parallel* axis passing through the centroid gives

$$\bar{h} = \frac{I_0 + Ah_c{}^2}{Ah_c}$$

where I_0 is the moment of inertia of the area about a horizontal axis through the centroid.

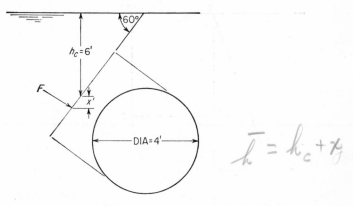

Fig. 2·14

Now if the center of pressure is a vertical distance x below the centroid, so that $\bar{h} = h_c + x$,

$$h_c + x = \frac{I_0}{Ah_c} + h_c$$

Therefore
$$x = \frac{I_0}{Ah_c} \tag{2·10}$$

Example: Calculate the magnitude, direction, and point of action of the resultant force on one side of a circular disk immersed in water at an inclination of 60° with its center 6 ft below the surface, as shown in Fig. 2·14.

The magnitude of the force is

$$\gamma h_c A = 62.4 \times 6 \times 4\pi = 4{,}710 \text{ lb}$$

The direction of the force is normal to the plane. The distance of the center of pressure below the centroid is given by

$$x = \frac{I_0}{Ah_c} = \frac{\pi d^4/64}{\pi d^2 \times \frac{6}{4}} = 0.167 \text{ ft}$$

Therefore, $\bar{h} = h_c + x = 6.167$ ft below the surface. Or alternatively, the center of pressure is $0.167/\sin 60°$ or 0.192 ft downward along the area below the centroid.

2·6   The forces on submerged curved surfaces

Consider the curved surface AB shown in Fig. 2·15. The net horizontal force on this curved section is the same as the force on the

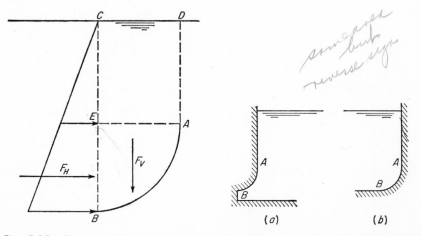

Fig. 2·15. Forces acting on a curved submerged area.

Fig. 2·16. Forces acting on curved submerged areas.

section EB (i.e., pressure $\times$ projected area), and it acts through the center of pressure of EB. The methods developed in Arts. 2·4 and 2·5 may be used to evaluate this force.

Since no shear can exist across CB or DA, *the weight of the fluid enclosed by $ABCD$ must be supported by the surface AB and is thus the vertical force applied to AB. It acts through the center of gravity of $ABCD$.*

The resultant force may now be calculated from these two. It should be noted that both the vertical and horizontal forces are the same on both sides of AB, although they act in different directions. Hence the forces acting on AB in Fig. 2·16a and b have the same magnitude, and those in (a) may be calculated by using the data shown in (b) and reversing the sign.

Example: Find the magnitude and direction of the force acting on the curved portion of the water tank shown in Fig. 2·17.

For the horizontal force F_H,

$$F_H = \text{pressure at centroid of } OB \times OB \times 3$$
$$= 5.5 \times 62.4 \times 3 \times 3$$
$$= 3,090 \text{ lb}$$

And for the vertical force F_V,

$$F_V = \text{weight of water above } AB$$
$$= \left(4 \times 3 + \frac{\pi 3^2}{4}\right) \times 3 \times 62.4$$
$$= 3,560 \text{ lb}$$

Hence the net force $R = \sqrt{3,090^2 + 3,560^2} = 4,700 \text{ lb}.$

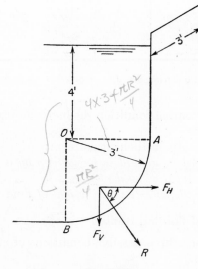

Fig. 2·17

Since AB is circular, the resultant, being normal to the surface, must pass through O at an angle θ to the horizontal given by

$$\tan \theta = \frac{F_V}{F_H} = \frac{3,560}{3,090}$$
$$\theta = 49°$$

2·7   Buoyancy and flotation

Following from Art. 2·6, the principles of Archimedes, with which the reader is probably familiar, may be rapidly deduced.

The vertical force acting downward on the immersed body shown in Fig. 2·18 is the weight of fluid contained in the volume $ABDEC$. The vertical force acting upward on the body is the same as the weight of liquid which would be contained in the volume $ABDFC$ in the absence of the body. *Thus there is a net upward force called buoyancy, equal to the weight of fluid displaced by the body.*

If the body is less dense than the fluid, then this buoyant force is larger than the weight, and the body will rise to the surface, if allowed

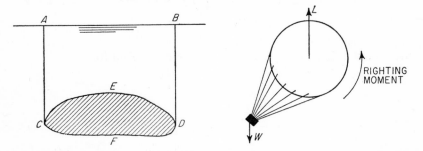

Fig. 2·18.   Buoyant force on an immersed solid.   Fig. 2·19.   A positively stable system.

to, and float. In the floating condition the buoyant force and the weight are exactly equal.

Restating these results in their usual form:

1. *A body immersed in a fluid is buoyed up by a force equal to the weight of fluid displaced by the body.*

2. *A floating body displaces its own weight of fluid in which it floats.*

2·8   The stability of floating bodies

A floating body has three possible conditions of stability: positive, neutral, or negative.

Positive stability. A body with positive stability will tend to return to its equilibrium position when slightly disturbed.

An aerostatic balloon, as shown in Fig. 2·19, has positive stability. The lifting force is located at the center of the balloon and acts vertically upward. The load is carried in the gondola and acts vertically downward. When the balloon is displaced from the upright position, say by a gust of wind, the resulting moment is seen to be a righting one, and so the balloon will return to its original position.

Neutral stability. A system in which the buoyant force and the weight are always vertically in line has neutral stability. In this condition the body may be moved to any position, and it will remain in this position.

Consider, for example, a floating ball as shown in Fig. 2·20. Displacement of the ball through any number of degrees will not change the position or value of the forces acting, and therefore no resulting moment can occur.

Negative stability. A system in which a small displacement from the equilibrium will cause the system to overturn has negative stability. Figure 2·21 shows a ship with a small hull and a tall mast very heavily

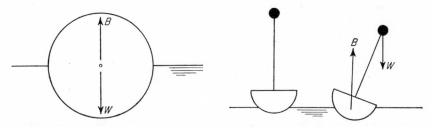

Fig. 2·20.   A neutrally stable system.   Fig. 2·21.   A negatively stable system.

weighted at the top. A small deflection from the vertical will result in an overturning moment, and the ship will capsize.

2·9 Metacentric height

In shipbuilding it is usual to have the center of buoyancy of the hull below the center of gravity (c.g.). By designing the hull cross section accordingly, any desired rolling stability may be obtained.

In the simple example shown in Fig. 2·22, the hull is assumed to be rectangular, and the ship is seen rolled through an angle θ.

The ship rolls about a point level with the waterline, since the shaded areas are the same, resulting in no increase of displacement. (This is the case for all ships with vertical sides when rolled through small angles.) The distribution of the displacement is changed, however, since there is a larger submerged area on one side than on the other, causing the center of buoyancy to move from B to B'.

The center of gravity, of course, remains on the center line, and the resulting moment is a righting one for a properly designed hull. *The distance GM between the center of gravity and the point where the ship's center line cuts the vertical through the center of buoyancy when θ is small is called the metacentric height.* It is a direct measure of the stability of the hull; the more stable the hull, the larger the value of the metacentric height. A zero value for the metacentric height would indicate neutral stability and a negative value, instability.

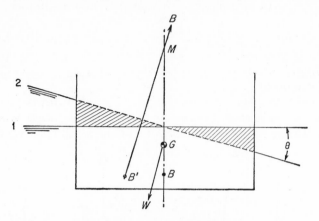

Fig. 2·22.   Metacentric height.

2·10   Static fluid masses subjected to acceleration

In this section it is important that the concept of a static fluid mass under acceleration be understood. Static fluid implies one in which all the fluid particles are at rest relative to one another, although the fluid as a whole may be moving. To achieve this, a completely static fluid must be subjected to a constant acceleration. There will be an unsteady period during which equilibrium is being established, and thereafter the fluid will be static. This final steady equilibrium condition is considered here.

There are three types of acceleration to consider—vertical, horizontal, and radial—the latter being called a forced vortex. This must not be confused with a free vortex, which is a fluid dynamic effect and so dealt with in the next chapter.

Vertical accelerations. Accelerating a tank of fluid vertically will not cause any change of the fluid position, the surface remaining horizontal.

Now consider a column of a vertically accelerated fluid as shown in Fig. 2·23. The vertical accelerating force on the column is

$$pA - W$$

and this is causing an upward vertical acceleration of a ft/sec². Therefore

$$pA - W = \frac{W}{g} a$$

But $W = hA\gamma$. Therefore

$$pA - hA\gamma = \frac{hA\gamma a}{g}$$

or

$$p = h\gamma \frac{a + g}{g} \qquad (2\cdot11)$$

which shows that for a constant acceleration *the pressure intensity at a point is still a linear function of the depth of the fluid.*

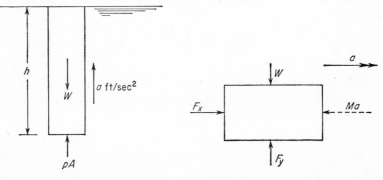

Fig. 2·23. Fluid mass under vertical acceleration.

Fig. 2·24. Fluid mass under horizontal acceleration.

Example: A tank containing 2 ft of water is accelerated vertically upward at 8 ft/sec². Estimate the horizontal force on a 6-ft length of one side of the tank.

The force on the side of the tank is given by

F = vertical area × pressure at depth of centroid of area
  = 6 × 2 × pressure at depth of 1 ft
  $= 12 \times 62.4 \dfrac{32.2 + 8}{32.2}$ (eq. 2-11)
  = 935 lb

Horizontal accelerations. Accelerating a tank of fluid horizontally will cause the fluid level at the front of the tank to fall and that at the rear to rise. If the acceleration is kept constant, the fluid will reach a stable equilibrium position. Now consider the forces acting on a small element of this stable fluid, as shown in Fig. 2·24.

The surrounding fluid exerts a force which can be considered a vertical component F_y and a horizontal component F_x. The weight of the element W acts downward, and the inertia force Ma acts to the left.

Resolving these forces horizontally and vertically yields

$$F_x = Ma = \frac{W}{g} a$$

$$F_y = W = Mg$$

Consider an element in the surface of the fluid. The net force exerted on it by the surrounding fluid must be normal to the surface; therefore, the surface at that point would make an angle with the horizontal so that

$$\tan \theta = \frac{F_x}{F_y} = \frac{Ma}{Mg} = \frac{a}{g} \qquad (2 \cdot 12)$$

This is a constant for any part of the surface; therefore, *the fluid surface will be straight and inclined at a constant angle to the horizontal,* as shown in Fig. 2·25.

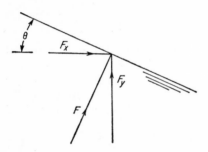

Fig. 2·25.   Free surface under horizontal acceleration.

Now the pressure intensity at any point may be calculated by using the relationship

$$p = \gamma h$$

and the forces on the ends of the tank F_1 and F_2 may be evaluated. As a check, the difference between the end forces F_1 and F_2 (Fig. 2·26) equals the accelerating force:

$$F_1 - F_2 = Ma$$

Example: An open horizontal tank 2 ft high, 2 ft wide, and 4 ft long is full of water. How much water is spilled when the tank is accelerated horizontally at 8.05 ft/sec² in a direction parallel with its longest side? What are the forces on the ends under these conditions?

The surface will incline at an angle θ to the horizontal so that

$$\tan \theta = \frac{a}{g} = \frac{1}{4}$$

$$\frac{8.05}{32.2} = \frac{1}{4}$$

The water will spill until the level at the rear of the tank just reaches the top of the tank and the surface is inclined at an angle of arctan

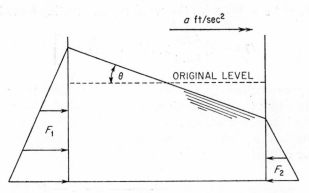

Fig. 2·26.   An open tank under horizontal acceleration.

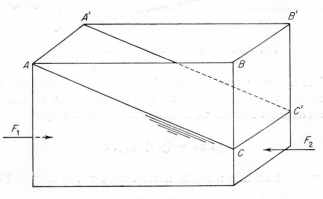

Fig. 2·27

$\frac{1}{4}$ to the horizontal. The quantity spilled is the volume of the wedge $ABCA'B'C'$, as shown in Fig. 2·27. Now

$$\frac{BC}{4} = \tan \theta = \frac{1}{4} \quad \text{constant}$$

and therefore $BC = 1$ ft

The volume spilled, then, is 4 ft³.

The pressure force on the rear face is given by the area multiplied by the pressure at the centroid. Therefore

$$F_1 = 2 \times 2 \times 1 \times 62.4 = 250 \text{ lb}$$

and similarly

$$F_2 = 2 \times 1 \times \tfrac{1}{2} \times 62.4 = 62.4 \text{ lb}$$

[Check: $F_1 - F_2 = 187.6$ lb; the required accelerating force is

$$(16 - 4) \frac{62.4}{32.2} \times 8.05 = 187.4 \text{ lb}\Big]$$

Radial acceleration. Radial acceleration is applied to a static fluid (i.e., one in which the fluid particles are at rest relative to one another) by rotating it in a vertical cylindrical container about its vertical axis with a constant angular velocity. This causes the fluid to rise toward the outside edge of the container.

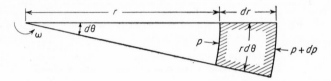

Fig. 2·28. Fluid mass under radial acceleration.

Consider a small element of a fluid of unit depth, rotating at a constant angular velocity ω as shown in Fig. 2·28. In a horizontal sense the forces acting outward on the element are given by

$$pr \, d\theta - (p + dp)r \, d\theta$$

and these must sustain a radial acceleration of $r\omega^2$ toward the center of rotation. Hence

$$pr \, d\theta - (p + dp)r \, d\theta = -r\omega^2 r \, d\theta \, dr \, \frac{\gamma}{g}$$

which reduces to

$$\frac{dp}{dr} = \omega^2 r \, \frac{\gamma}{g} \tag{2·13}$$

Since all the terms on the right-hand side of the equation are positive, it is apparent that *pressure is increasing with radius.*

Integrating this between the center of rotation ($r = 0$, $p = p_o$) and any general radius r, where the pressure is p,

integrated

$$\int_{p_o}^{p} dp = \gamma \int_{0}^{r} \frac{\omega^2 r}{g} \, dr$$

Therefore

$$p - p_o = \frac{\omega^2 \gamma}{g} \left[\frac{r^2}{2} \right]_0^r$$

or

$$\frac{p - p_o}{\gamma} = \frac{\omega^2 r^2}{2g} \qquad (2{\cdot}14)$$

Now the left-hand side of Eq. (2·13) has units of length and represents a head of fluid. This term can be replaced by y, which is the height of the fluid above the central height, yielding

$$y = \frac{\omega^2 r^2}{2g} \qquad \text{a parabola} \qquad (2{\cdot}15)$$

This is shown in Fig. 2·29. The pressure at any point can now be determined by using the relationship $p = \gamma h$.

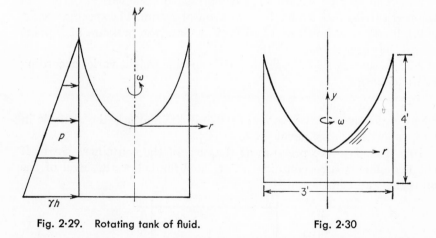

Fig. 2·29.   Rotating tank of fluid.   Fig. 2·30

Example: A cylinder of radius 1.5 ft and height 4 ft is rotated at 10 rad/sec about its vertical axis. If the cylinder was originally full of water, how much is spilled, and what is the pressure intensity at the center of the base of the cylinder? (See Fig. 2·30.)

From Eq. (2·15)

$$y_{max} = \frac{\omega^2 r_{max}^2}{2g}$$

$$= \frac{100 \times 1.5^2}{64.4}$$

$$= 3.5 \text{ ft}$$

The volume spilled is the volume of the paraboloid (equal to half the volume of the surrounding cylinder), or

$$\frac{\pi}{2} \times 1.5^2 \times 3.5 = 12.4 \text{ ft}^3$$

The pressure intensity at the center of the base of the cylinder is that due to a head of water of 0.5 ft. Therefore

$$p = 0.5 \times 62.4 = 31.2 \text{ psf}$$

PROBLEMS

2·1   Calculate the gage pressure at a depth of 200 ft in seawater. What is this pressure in inches of mercury absolute? (Take barometric pressure as 30 in. of mercury.)

2·2   The specific weight of a compressible fluid varies directly as the vertical distance from a fixed horizontal datum. The specific weight is 0.1 lb/ft³ at a depth of 1,800 ft. Calculate the pressure at a point where the specific weight is 0.06 lb/ft³.

2·3   Assuming that the atmospheric specific weight varies according to the equation

$$\gamma = \gamma_o e^{-h/28,000}$$

where γ_o is the sea-level value of 0.076 lb/ft³ and h is the altitude in feet, calculate the sea-level pressure in psi.

2·4   Calculate the pressure at the base of the container shown. If the manometer tube contains water, how far below the level of the oil is the water in the tube?

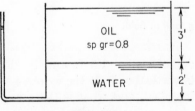

Prob. 2·4

2·5   Calculate the reading of the gage shown in the figure.

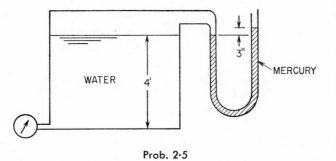

Prob. 2·5

2·6   Taking 14.7 psi as atmospheric pressure, complete the following
table.

psia	psig	in. of mercury, absolute	ft of water, absolute	ft of water, gage
14.7				
	34			
		16		
			55	
				−7

2·7   Calculate the reading of the gage A in the figure.

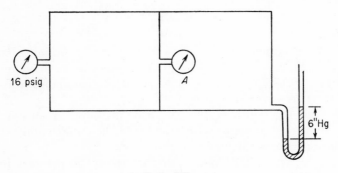

Prob. 2·7

2·8 Calculate the pressure at A in the figure.

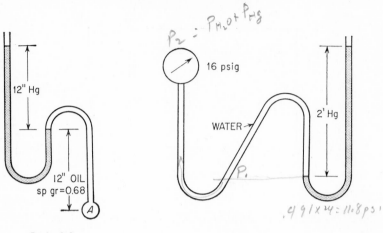

$P_2 = P_{H_2O} + P_{Hg}$

16 psig

WATER

P_2

2' Hg

P_1

12" Hg

12" OIL
sp gr = 0.68

A

.4 9/ × 4 = 11.8 psi

Prob. 2·8   **Prob. 2·9**

2·9 Calculate the distance of the gage below the top of the mercury column.

2·10 A differential U-tube manometer containing mercury is connected between two pressure sources with pressures of 72 psig and 6 in. of mercury vacuum respectively. What is the measured difference in levels in the two arms of the manometer?

2·11 If the manometer of Prob. 2·10 is tilted at an angle of 60° to the vertical, what will be the inclined difference in levels in the arms of the manometer?

2·12 A very small pressure difference is measured with an enlarged-ended U-tube manometer containing oil (sp gr = 0.82) and water. The large ends are 2 in. in diameter, and the tube bore is 0.197 in. If the common surface in the tube is seen to fall 3.5 in., what is the applied pressure?

2·13 An enlarged-ended U-tube manometer containing two immiscible fluids (sp gr = 0.8 and 0.91) has ends of 1-in. diameter and a tube bore of 0.197 in. What movement of the common level will be caused by a pressure difference of 0.04 psi?

2·14 Find the depth of the center of pressure for an equilateral triangle immersed in water with an edge in the surface and the plane of the triangle perpendicular to the surface.

2.15 The gate is 12 ft long. Calculate the water pressure force on the gate and the position of the center of pressure.

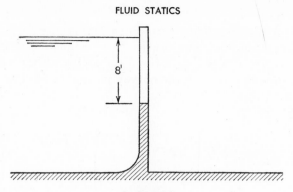

Prob. 2·15

2·16 Calculate the pressure force on the dam face and the position of the center of pressure.

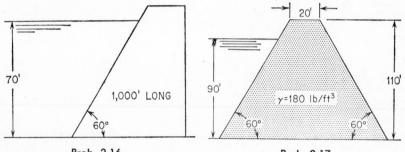

Prob. 2·16   Prob. 2·17

2·17 The dam is 100 ft long. Calculate the resultant force on the dam and its position and direction.

2·18 Estimate the height h of water that will cause the gate to open. Neglect the weight of the gate.

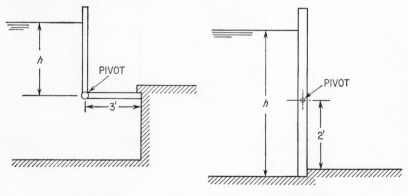

Prob. 2·18   Prob. 2·19

2·19   Estimate the height h of water that will cause the gate to open.

2·20   A seagoing ship's hull consists of a rectangle with a semicircle drawn on the lower edge. Find the force acting on the two vertical sides and also that acting on the curved portion of the hull if the hull is 70 ft long.

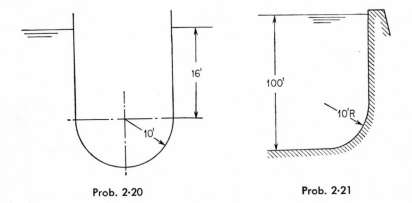

Prob. 2·20   Prob. 2·21

2·21   A dam 300 ft long has a vertical face with a circular foot as shown. Find the force on the curved portion.

2·22   Calculate the total pressure force on a 1-ft length of this dam.

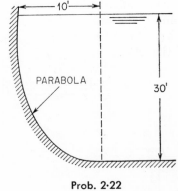

Prob. 2·22

2·23   A tank truck has an elliptical tank 8 ft wide and 4 ft deep. Calculate the pressure force acting on a lower quadrant of this tank if the tank is 18 ft long and contains water.

2·24   Calculate the net force acting on the cone shown in the figure. The fluid is water.

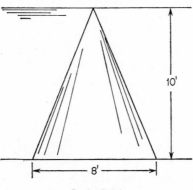

Prob. 2·24

2·25   A ship weighing 80,000 lb has vertical sides and a draft of 4 ft in fresh water. What will be the draft in seawater?

2·26   If a cargo weighing 20,000 lb is placed in the ship of Prob. 2·25, what would be the drafts in fresh and salt water?

2·27   A submarine has a total volume of 1,700 ft³ and a weight of 80,000 lb. How much seawater must be pumped in to keep the submarine submerged?

2·28   What volumetric displacement would be required to float a seaplane of 5,000-lb weight in seawater?

2·29   An aircraft gravity-feed fuel tank is mounted 2 ft above and 8 ft behind the carburetor. What is the maximum level acceleration that the aircraft can attain without suffering fuel starvation?

2·30   What is the maximum level acceleration that can be applied to this tank without causing the liquid to spill?

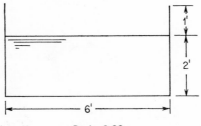

Prob. 2·30

2·31   A tank 8 ft long, 2 ft deep, and 3 ft wide, originally full of liquid, is accelerated horizontally at 16.1 ft/sec². How much liquid is spilled, and what are the forces on each end of the tank under these conditions? (The liquid has a specific gravity of 0.9.)

2·32   A rocket fuel tank containing nitric acid ($\gamma = 80$ lb/ft³) consists of a vertical cylinder 2 ft in diameter and 7 ft long. What is the pressure force on the base of the tank when, with the tank full, the rocket is fired with a vertical acceleration of $5g$?

At a point in the flight when the tank is half empty, the acceleration is $7.5g$ vertically upward. What is the pressure at the base of the tank under these conditions?

2·33   Calculate the pressure force on each end of a tank 2 ft wide and containing 3 ft of water when (a) accelerated vertically upward at 10 ft/sec², and (b) accelerated vertically downward at 7 ft/sec².

2·34   An upright cylindrical tank 3 ft in diameter and containing oil of sp gr = 0.87 is spun about its vertical axis at 200 rpm so that the depth of fluid at the center of the tank is 1 ft. Calculate the pressure intensity at the foot of the vertical sides. At what rotational speed would the depth of fluid at the center be zero, assuming that none is spilled?

2·35   An upright cylindrical tank of 1-ft radius contains 1 ft of water. Calculate the pressure intensity at the foot of the vertical edge when rotated at 100 rpm.

CHAPTER 3

The Flow of Incompressible Fluids

The large number of variables involved in predicting the behavior of a fluid in motion makes it impossible to analyze that motion without assuming some degree of simplification.

The degree of simplification allowable depends upon the required accuracy of the result and the validity of the assumptions made. For instance, it is reasonable to assume incompressibility for water under most circumstances, but air must often be considered a very compressible fluid.

Viscosity often causes great mathematical difficulty in analysis, and for this reason the concept of an ideal fluid is introduced. An ideal fluid is one that has zero viscosity and therefore will not support a shear force of any kind. Results obtained from consideration of an ideal fluid often vary considerably from the observed behavior of a real fluid, and care must be exercised when deciding whether the assumption of an ideal fluid may be justified.

In this chapter the flow of both real and ideal fluids will be considered, but incompressibility will be assumed throughout.

3·1 Steady and unsteady flow

Fluid flow may be steady or unsteady. If at any point in a flow *any* variable changes with time, then the flow is unsteady. Conversely, if at any point in a flow all the variables remain constant with time, then the flow is steady.

Consider a fixed point in a water pipe downstream from a closed valve. At this point the velocity is zero. At time t_1 the valve is opened, and the velocity at the considered point changes as shown in Fig. 3·1. Between times t_1 and t_2 the flow is changing and therefore unsteady. After time t_2 the flow is fully established and has become steady.

The treatment of unsteady flows is beyond the scope of this text; hence, only steady flows will be considered.

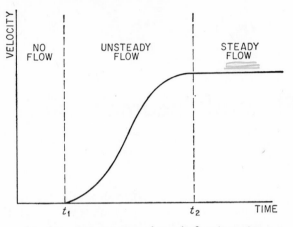

Fig. 3·1.   Development of steady flow in a pipe.

3·2   The streamline and the streamtube

If a line is drawn in a flow in such a manner that any tangent to the line is in the direction of the velocity of the flow at the tangency point, then that line is a *streamline*. These streamlines are very useful in obtaining a visual interpretation of a flow pattern.

Since the streamline is at all points parallel to the surrounding flow, it is apparent that there can be no flow across it. Streamlines in an accelerating flow will therefore become closer together, whereas in a decelerating flow they will spread apart.

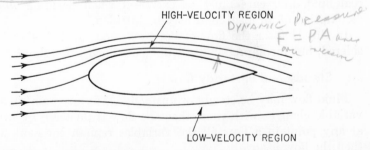

Fig. 3·2.   Streamline representation of flow over an airfoil.

Figure 3·2 shows the flow past a lifting airfoil. Notice that on the top surface of the wing, a high-velocity area is shown with the streamlines close together and that on the lower surface of the wing, the low-velocity area is shown with the streamlines farther apart.

If, in a three-dimensional flow, a closed loop is drawn and a stream-line drawn through each point of that loop, a *streamtube* is generated (Fig. 3·3). Since there can be no flow across a streamline, it follows that there can be no flow across the walls of a streamtube.

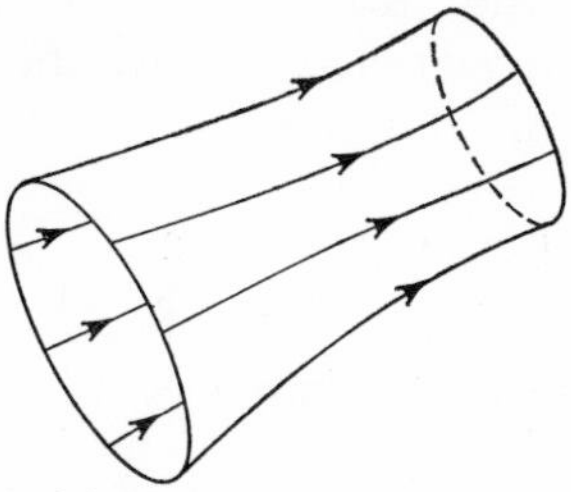

Fig. 3·3.   A streamtube.

3·3   One-, two-, and three-dimensional flows

One-dimensional flow is that in which the behavior of each and every streamline is the same and all the streamlines are parallel. The flow may be considered to have only one dimension, i.e., along a streamline, since any streamline will be representative of them all. The flow through a pipe or channel is one-dimensional (see Fig. 3·4a).

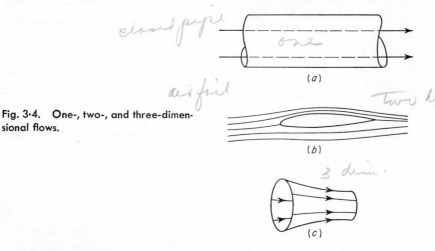

Fig. 3·4.   One-, two-, and three-dimen-sional flows.

The flow across an infinitely long airfoil is considered two-dimensional. The flow pattern shown in Fig. 3·4b is the same at any cross section of the airfoil and may be regarded as representative of the whole airfoil. The streamlines are everywhere parallel with the plane of the page.

Any flow in which the streamlines are nowhere parallel is a three-dimensional flow. Figure 3·4c shows the streamlines of a flow entering a nozzle; since the streamlines are never parallel, the flow is three-dimensional.

3·4   The equation of continuity

Consider the steady-flow streamtube shown in Fig. 3·5. The flow is entering at section 1 and leaving at section 2. There is no flow across the tube wall; and since the flow is steady, there is no accumulation

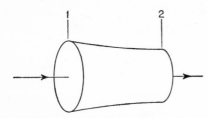

Fig. 3·5.   Steady-flow streamtube.

of fluid taking place within the streamtube. It is necessary, then, that the amount of fluid entering section 1 in a given time be equal to the amount of fluid leaving section 2 in the same time.

If the velocity, fluid density, and tube cross-sectional area at stations 1 and 2 are $V_1 \rho_1 A_1$ and $V_2 \rho_2 A_2$ respectively, then

$$\rho_1 A_1 V_1 = \rho_2 A_2 V_2$$

or $\rho A V = \text{const} = G$, the mass flow rate   **(3·1)**

This is the *equation of continuity*. For incompressible flow (i.e., $\rho = $ constant), it reduces to

$$A V = \text{const} = Q, \text{ the flow rate} \qquad \textbf{(3·2)}$$

3·5   Euler's equation of motion

Euler's equation is most easily established by considering a small element of fluid enclosed in a streamtube.

The element shown in Fig. 3·6 has a mean cross-sectional area of A and a mean periphery of P. Its length is ds, and the centroid of its downstream face is dz higher than the centroid of its upstream face.

There is a frictional shear stress of τ acting at the walls of the tube and, hence, a frictional retarding force of $\tau P \, ds$ owing to this stress.

The net pressure on the element in the downstream direction is

$$(p + dp) - p = dp$$

and therefore, the pressure force acting on the element is $A \, dp$. The total resistive force on the element is then

$$A \, dp + \tau P \, ds$$

and so the work done in moving fluid from station 1 to station 2 against this force is $(A \, dp + \tau P \, ds) \, ds$.

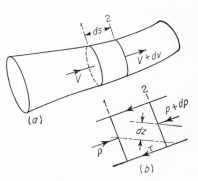

Fig. 3·6. (a) A small fluid element within a streamtube. (b) Detail of the element.

The gain in kinetic energy in moving from station 1 to station 2 is

$$\tfrac{1}{2}\rho A \, ds \, [(V + dV)^2 - V^2] = \tfrac{1}{2}\rho A \, ds \, (2V \, dV + dV^2)$$
$$= \rho A V \, dV \, ds$$

when terms in dV^2 are neglected. The gain in potential energy is

$$\rho A \, ds \, g \, dz$$

Since no external energy has been added, the work done and the energy gained must sum to zero. Thus

$$(A \, dp + \tau P \, ds) \, ds + \rho A V \, dV \, ds + \rho A g \, ds \, dz = 0$$

which, on division by $\rho A g \, ds$, gives

$$\frac{dp}{\rho g} + \frac{\tau P \, ds}{\rho g A} + \frac{V \, dV}{g} + dz = 0$$

But $\rho g = \gamma$, and A/P is defined as the *hydraulic radius R;* hence

$$\frac{dp}{\gamma} + \frac{\tau \, ds}{\gamma R} + \frac{V \, dV}{g} + dz = 0 \qquad \textbf{(3·3)}$$

which is *Euler's equation of motion.* For ideal fluids, $\tau = 0$, and Eq. (3·3) reduces to

$$\frac{dp}{\gamma} + \frac{V \, dV}{g} + dz = 0 \qquad (3·4)$$

It is important to remember that since Eqs. (3·3) and (3·4) were established by considering the flow within a streamtube, they apply only to flow within a streamtube or along a streamline.

3·6 Bernoulli's equation

Integration of Eq. (3·4) yields *Bernoulli's equation*, one of the most useful tools of fluid mechanics.

$$\int_1^2 \frac{dp}{\gamma} + \int_1^2 \frac{V\,dV}{g} + \int_1^2 dz = 0$$

Therefore

$$\frac{p_2 - p_1}{\gamma} + \frac{V_2{}^2 - V_1{}^2}{2g} + (z_2 - z_1) = 0$$

assuming that γ is constant. Hence

$$\frac{p_1}{\gamma} + \frac{V_1{}^2}{2g} + z_1 = \frac{p_2}{\gamma} + \frac{V_2{}^2}{2g} + z_2 \tag{3·5}$$

or

$$\frac{p}{\gamma} + \frac{V^2}{2g} + z = \text{const} \tag{3·6}$$

This equation stated in words means that the sum of the pressure energy, the velocity or kinetic energy, and the potential energy of an *ideal incompressible* fluid is a constant along a streamline.

In Bernoulli's equation, as derived above, the quantity z is referred to as the potential head of the fluid. Since the pressure and velocity terms also have units of length, it is usual to refer to them as the *pressure head* and the *velocity head*. They are shown diagrammatically in Fig. 3·7. Notice that the total energy line is horizontal, parallel to the potential datum. If the fluid is not ideal and exhibits frictional effects, a gradual loss of total energy appears.

Example 1: A 3-in.-diameter fire hose contains water flowing at a rate of 3 cfs. If the pressure within the pipe is 10 psig, what is the maximum height to which the water may be sprayed?

In this problem all the energy of the water is to be converted into potential energy. The velocity and the pressure will both be zero at the maximum height.

The original pressure energy is given by

$$\frac{p}{\gamma} = \frac{10 \times 144}{62.4} = 23.1 \text{ ft}$$

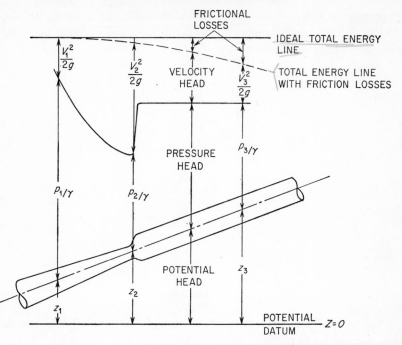

Fig. 3·7.　Head variations through an irregular tube.

The velocity of the water in the hose may be obtained from the equation of continuity, $Q = AV$.

$$3 = \frac{\pi \times 3^2 V}{4 \times 12^2}$$

Hence

$$V = 3 \times \frac{64}{\pi} = 61.05 \text{ fps}$$

Thus the kinetic energy of the flow is

$$\frac{61.05^2}{2 \times 32.2} = 57.9 \text{ ft}$$

Defining the level of the hose as the potential energy datum, the total energy is

$$23.1 + 57.9 + 0 = 81.0 \text{ ft}$$

and this is the height to which the water may be sprayed.

Example 2: Water is flowing upward through the contraction shown in Fig. 3·8. A manometer records the pressure difference $p_B - p_A$ as shown. Calculate the flow rate.

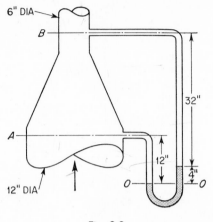

Fig. 3·8

The pressure in each arm of the U-tube at level O-O is the same. On the left-hand side the pressure is

$$p_A + 12 \text{ in. of water}$$

and on the right-hand side the pressure is

$$p_B + 4 \text{ in. of mercury} + 32 \text{ in. of water}$$

Therefore $p_A - p_B = 4$ in. mercury $+ (32 - 12)$ in. water

Hence $$\frac{p_A - p_B}{\gamma} = \frac{4 \times 13.55 + 20}{12} = 6.18 \text{ ft}$$

Now $z_A - z_B = -2$ ft and from the equation of continuity

$$V_A \frac{\pi}{4} = V_B \frac{\pi}{4} \left(\frac{1}{2}\right)^2$$

or $$V_A = \frac{V_B}{4}$$

Applying Bernoulli's equation for an incompressible ideal fluid,

$$\frac{p_A - p_B}{\gamma} + \frac{V_A{}^2 - V_B{}^2}{2g} + (z_A - z_B) = 0$$

or
$$6.18 + \frac{V_B{}^2(\frac{1}{4} - 1)}{2g} - 2 = 0$$

i.e.,
$$\frac{3V_B{}^2}{8g} = 4.18$$

Hence
$$V_B = 19 \text{ fps}$$
and therefore
$$Q = A_B V_B = 3.73 \text{ cfs}$$

3·7 Derivations from Bernoulli's equation

Torricelli's theorem. Applying Bernoulli's equation to the flow from a large reservoir, it is possible to reduce the velocity and pressure to zero at a point on the surface of the reservoir.

At station 1 on the streamline shown in Fig. 3·9, the velocity may be considered zero if the tank is sufficiently large. Since station 1 lies on the fluid surface, the pressure at this point is zero (gage).

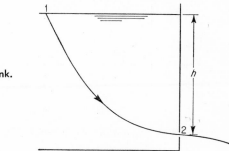

Fig. 3·9. Flow from a large tank.

The pressure in an open fluid jet must be atmospheric (i.e., zero gage) since there are no walls to restrain a different pressure; thus $p_1 = V_1 = p_2 = 0$.

Applying Bernoulli's equation between stations 1 and 2 gives

$$z_1 = \frac{V_2{}^2}{2g} + z_2$$

or
$$V_2{}^2 = 2g(z_1 - z_2)$$

But $z_1 - z_2 = h$, the applied head; hence

$$V_2 = \sqrt{2gh} \tag{3·7}$$

This is *Torricelli's theorem*. If the area of the jet in Fig. 3·9 is A square units, then the flow rate leaving the tank is

$$Q = A\sqrt{2gh} \tag{3·8}$$

Example: Find the distance x that the jet from the tank of Fig. 3·10 will travel horizontally before impinging on the floor.

From Torricelli's theorem

$$V = \sqrt{2gh} = 11.35 \text{ fps}$$

In a vertical sense, the fluid starts from rest and falls a distance of s ft under the acceleration due to gravity; thus

$$s = \frac{gt^2}{2}$$

so the time taken to fall 2 ft is $\sqrt{2s/g}$ or 0.353 sec. During this time

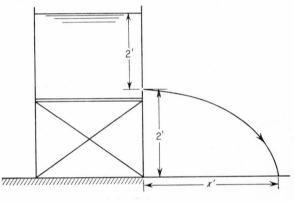

Fig. 3·10

the fluid will travel a horizontal distance of

$$11.35 \times 0.353 = 4 \text{ ft}$$

The energy equation for systems to which external energy is added. It was seen in Art. 3·6 that the units of each term of the incompressible form of Bernoulli's equation were units of length, usually feet.

Now the energy content of a fluid can be measured in units of ft-lb/lb, and these units have the same dimensions as the terms of Bernoulli's equation. It is possible to say, then, that p/γ represents the pressure head of a fluid or the *pressure energy contained per pound of fluid*, and similarly for the velocity and potential heads.

For a system in which a machine, such as a pump or turbine, is adding or subtracting energy from the system at a rate of E ft-lb/lb of fluid flowing, Bernoulli's equation can be applied, provided that an extra term is added to account for the external energy. Thus, for the system shown in Fig. 3·11,

$$\frac{p_1}{\gamma} + \frac{V_1^2}{2g} + z_1 + E = \frac{p_2}{\gamma} + \frac{V_2^2}{2g} + z_2 \qquad (3\cdot9)$$

Example: A hydraulic turbine operates from a water supply with a 200-ft head above the turbine inlet, as shown in Fig. 3·12. It discharges the water to atmosphere through a 12-in.-diameter duct, with a velocity of 45 fps. Calculate the horsepower output of the turbine.

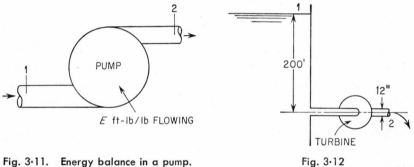

Fig. 3·11.   Energy balance in a pump.   Fig. 3·12

If E is the energy extracted per pound of fluid flowing, then the energy equation may be written as

$$\frac{p_1}{\gamma} + \frac{V_1^2}{2g} + z_1 = E + \frac{p_2}{\gamma} + \frac{V_2^2}{2g} + z_2$$

where suffix 1 refers to a point upstream of the turbine and suffix 2 to a point downstream of the turbine.

If the exit from the turbine is defined as the potential datum, then $z_2 = 0$ and

$$\frac{p_1}{\gamma} + \frac{V_1^2}{2g} + z_1 = 200 \text{ ft-lb/lb}$$

Therefore $$200 = E + \frac{p_2}{\gamma} + \frac{V_2^2}{2g}$$

Now since the discharge is to atmosphere, $p_2 = 0$. Hence

$$200 = E + \frac{45^2}{2g}$$

Thus $$E = 200 - 31.3 = 168.7 \text{ ft-lb/lb}$$

The rate of fluid flow is given by $Q = AV$ cfs, and the weight of fluid flowing by $Q\gamma$ lb/sec. Therefore the work done on the turbine is $EQ\gamma$ ft-lb/sec or

$$\frac{EQ\gamma}{550} \text{ hp} = \frac{168.7 \times \pi \times 45 \times 62.4}{4 \times 550}$$

$$= 675 \text{ hp}$$

The aerodynamic form of Bernoulli's equation (for incompressible ideal gas flow). Multiplying Eq. (3·6) through by γ gives

$$p + \frac{V^2\gamma}{2g} + z\gamma = \text{const} \tag{3·10}$$

The ratio γ/g is the density ρ, and for gases the quantity γz is negligible since the specific weight of gases is very small. Usually the change in potential z is also small in gas dynamic problems. Equation (3·10) then reduces to

$$p + \tfrac{1}{2}\rho V^2 = \text{const} \tag{3·11}$$

which is the aerodynamic form of Bernoulli's equation for ideal incompressible flow of gases.

In this equation p is referred to as the static pressure and $\rho V^2/2$ as the dynamic pressure. The units of both are pressure units, usually psf.

If at any point in a gas flow the velocity is reduced to zero, the point is referred to as a stagnation point, and the static pressure at this point is called the stagnation pressure p_s. This is the maximum pressure that may be recorded in a flow.

$$p_s = p_o + \tfrac{1}{2}\rho V_o^2 \tag{3·12}$$

where p_o = free stream static pressure
V_o = free stream velocity

Example: What is the maximum pressure exerted on an aircraft flying at 200 mph at sea level? ($\rho = 0.00238$ slug/ft³; $p_o = 14.7$ psi.)

The maximum pressure is at a stagnation point and is given by

$$p_s = 14.7 \times 144 + \tfrac{1}{2} \times 0.00238(200 \times {}^{88}\!/_{60})^2$$

$$= 2,220 \text{ psfa}$$

$$= 15.42 \text{ psia}$$

3·8 Flowmeters and suction devices

If the cross-sectional area of a flow changes reasonably rapidly, the flow rate can be calculated from pressures read at two points along the flow.

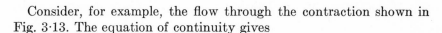

Fig. 3·13. A crude flowmeter.

Consider, for example, the flow through the contraction shown in Fig. 3·13. The equation of continuity gives

$$Q = A_1 V_1 = A_2 V_2 \tag{3·2}$$

and from Bernoulli's equation,

$$\frac{p_1}{\gamma} + z_1 + \frac{V_1{}^2}{2g} = \frac{p_2}{\gamma} + z_2 + \frac{V_2{}^2}{2g} \tag{3·5}$$

Now from these two equations

$$\frac{V_2{}^2}{2g} = \frac{p_1}{\gamma} + z_1 - \frac{p_2}{\gamma} - z_2 + \frac{V_1{}^2}{2g}$$

$$= \frac{p_1}{\gamma} + z_1 - \frac{p_2}{\gamma} - z_2 + \frac{(A_2 V_2 / A_1)^2}{2g}$$

so

$$\frac{V_2{}^2}{2g}\left[1 - \left(\frac{A_2}{A_1}\right)^2\right] = \frac{p_1}{\gamma} + z_1 - \frac{p_2}{\gamma} - z_2$$

or

$$V_2 = \sqrt{\frac{2g(p_1/\gamma + z_1 - p_2/\gamma - z_2)}{1 - (A_2/A_1)^2}}$$

Therefore

$$Q = A_2 \sqrt{\frac{2g(p_1/\gamma + z_1 - p_2/\gamma - z_2)}{1 - (A_2/A_1)^2}} \tag{3·13}$$

The venturi meter. It is not usually desirable to reduce the diameter of a pipe downstream of a flowmeter, and for this reason the simple contraction discussed above is seldom used. One of the two most common types of flow-measuring devices is the *venturi meter*. This is shown diagrammatically in Fig. 3·14.

It is basically a simple, smooth contraction with a diffusing section added to restore the pipe diameter to its original value. The included angle in the diffuser is kept to 6° or less to prevent flow breakaway

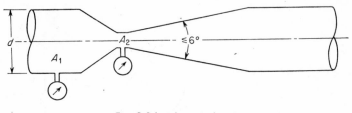

Fig. 3·14.   A venturi meter.

from the diffuser walls, causing large head losses in the meter. Pressure tappings are made in the upstream parallel-sided section of the meter and at the throat. The flow rate through the meter is given by

$$Q = C_v A_2 \sqrt{\frac{2g(p_1/\gamma + z_1 - p_2/\gamma - z_2)}{1 - (A_2/A_1)^2}}$$ (3·14)

where C_v is a constant for the meter. The value of C_v is determined experimentally for each meter and lies between 0.6 and 0.95 usually.

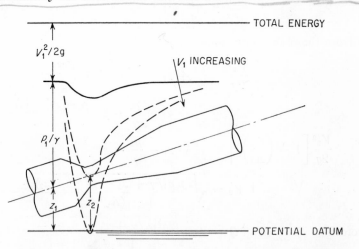

Fig. 3·15.   Pressure and velocity variation through a venturi meter.

Figure 3·15 shows the variation of pressure through a typical venturi tube. Notice that as the inlet velocity V_1 increases, the pressure at the throat p_2 decreases, eventually becoming negative. When the pressure in the throat becomes sufficiently small, so that

$$\frac{p_2}{\gamma} \leqslant -z_2$$

then fluid (of the same specific weight) can be sucked from the datum level by connecting a tube from the throat to the fluid at datum level, provided that the value of p_2 is not as low as the vapor pressure of the fluid—in which case the fluid would boil with unpredictable results.

Example: Water flows through a horizontal venturi meter with an inlet diameter of 4 in. and a throat diameter of 2 in. The pressure at the inlet end is 10 psig, and at the throat the pressure is 3 in. of mercury vacuum. Calculate the flow rate, given that the constant for the meter is 0.82.

Since the meter is horizontal, $z_1 = z_2 = 0$, say, and

$$Q = 0.82 A_2 \sqrt{\frac{2g(p_1/\gamma - p_2/\gamma)}{1 - (A_2/A_1)^2}}$$

Now $\quad \dfrac{p_1}{\gamma} = \dfrac{10 \times 144}{62.4}$ ft of water $\quad (= 10\ PSIG.)$

and $\quad \dfrac{p_2}{\gamma} = -\tfrac{3}{12} \times 13.55$ ft of water $\quad (Mercury\ 3''\ Vacuum.\ minus\ a\ minus = +)$

Hence $\quad Q = 0.82\,\dfrac{\pi}{4}\,\dfrac{4}{144}\sqrt{\dfrac{2g(1{,}440/62.4 + 3 \times 13.55/12)}{1 - \tfrac{1}{16}}}$

$\qquad = 0.0179\,\sqrt{68.7(23.1 + 3.39)}$

$\qquad = 0.765$ cfs

The orifice meter. Whereas the venturi meter is designed to have very low resistance to flow, it has a serious disadvantage in that the larger the value of A_1/A_2 and thus the more sensitive the meter, the longer the meter must be. Where space is limited, a second type of meter called the *orifice meter* is used.

This device is simply a plate with a sharp-edged hole in it placed in the pipe, as shown in Fig. 3·16. The flow rate through such a meter is given ideally by Eq. (3·13), where

A_1 = area of pipe upstream of orifice
A_2 = area of orifice

However, it is not possible to measure the pressure in the exact plane of the orifice, and so it must be measured a short distance downstream of the orifice. At this point the area of flow is given by $C_o A_2$, where

C_o is a constant for the meter, and the flow rate is given by

$$Q = C_o A_2 \sqrt{\frac{2g(p_1/\gamma + z_1 - p_2/\gamma - z_2)}{1 - C_o{}^2(A_2/A_1)^2}}$$

Now taking into account the losses inherent in the meter, the true flow rate is given by

$$Q = C_v C_o A_2 \sqrt{\frac{2g(p_1/\gamma + z_1 - p_2/\gamma - z_2)}{1 - C_o{}^2(A_2/A_1)^2}} \qquad \text{(3·15)}$$

where C_v is the loss coefficient for the meter.

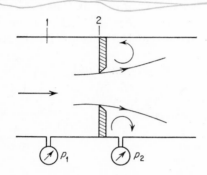

Fig. 3·16.   An orifice meter.

Evaluating the coefficients C_v and C_o is considerably more difficult than evaluating C_v for the venturi meter, but if the ratio d_2/d_1 is sufficiently small, say one-third or less, then

$$1 - C_o{}^2 \left(\frac{A_2}{A_1}\right)^2 \doteq 1$$

and the flow rate reduces to

$$Q = C_v C_o A_2 \sqrt{2g \left(\frac{p_1}{\gamma} + z_1 - \frac{p_2}{\gamma} - z_2\right)}$$

$$= k A_2 \sqrt{2g \left(\frac{p_1}{\gamma} + z_1 - \frac{p_2}{\gamma} - z_2\right)} \qquad \text{(3·16)}$$

where k is the overall constant for the meter.

The pitot-static tube. The pitot-static tube is a device for measuring flow velocities. It consists of two tubes, one within the other and sealed at the joints, as shown in Fig. 3·17. The inner or pitot tube is open at the end and, when pointing directly into the flow, records the total head of the flow, $p + \rho V^2/2$.

The outer or static tube has a number of holes drilled in it at right angles to the flow direction so that this tube records only the local static pressure p.

The difference between the two pressures thus obtained is the dynamic pressure $\rho V^2/2$, which can be converted into velocity if the density ρ is known.

The most common application of the pitot-static tube is aircraft velocity measurement. The two pressures are led into an airspeed indicator (ASI) which is calibrated directly in mph, assuming ρ to hav eits sea-level value of 0.00238 slug/ft³. At sea level, then, the

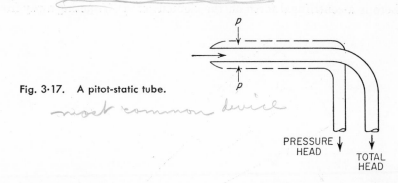

Fig. 3·17.   A pitot-static tube.

PRESSURE
HEAD

TOTAL
HEAD

indicated airspeed (IAS) will be the same as the true airspeed (TAS); but at altitudes where the air density is less than the sea-level value, the IAS will be less than the TAS. The advantage of this system will be explained in Chaps. 9 and 10.

Example: An aircraft flying at an altitude of 15,000 ft ($\rho = 0.00150$ slug/ft³) has an IAS of 350 mph. What is its TAS?

The ASI is recording the same dynamic pressure that it would record at sea level and 350 mph; therefore

$$\frac{\rho V^2}{2} = \frac{0.00238}{2}\left(350 \times \frac{88}{60}\right)^2 \text{ psf}$$

But at 15,000 ft $\rho = 0.00150$ slug/ft³; therefore

$$\tfrac{1}{2} \times 0.00150(v \times {}^{88}\!/_{60})^2 = \tfrac{1}{2} \times 0.00238(350 \times {}^{88}\!/_{60})^2$$

where v is the TAS in mph. Hence

$$v = \frac{0.00238}{0.00150} \times 350 = 512 \text{ mph}$$

3·9   Flow in a circular path

Figure 3·18 shows a small element of unit length flowing horizontally in a circular path about center O. The volume of this element is

$$r\,d\theta\,dr$$

and its mass is

$$\frac{\gamma}{g}\,r\,d\theta\,dr \qquad \text{slugs}$$

There is a centrifugal force on the element of mV^2/r acting away from

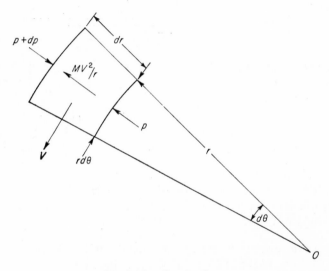

Fig. 3·18.   Circular flow.

the center of curvature, or

$$\frac{\gamma}{g}\,V^2\,d\theta\,dr$$

which is balanced by the pressure forces

$$(p + dp)r\,d\theta - pr\,d\theta$$

Hence

$$\frac{\gamma}{g}\,V^2\,d\theta\,dr = r\,d\theta\,dp$$

Thus

$$\frac{dp}{\gamma} = \frac{V^2}{rg}\,dr \qquad\qquad (3·17)$$

Now if terms in z are neglected, Eq. (3·4) reduces to

$$\frac{dp}{\gamma} = -\frac{V\,dV}{g}$$

Therefore

$$\frac{V^2}{rg}\,dr = -\frac{V\,dV}{g}$$

which reduces to

$$\frac{dV}{V} + \frac{dr}{r} = 0 \qquad (3·18)$$

Equation (3·18) is also obtainable by differentiating the equation

$$Vr = \text{const} \qquad \textbf{(3·19)}$$

which is then the *equation of motion of circular flow.*

Example: The wind velocity 5 miles from the center of a tornado was measured as 30 mph, and the barometer was read as 29 in. of mercury. Calculate the wind velocity ½ mile from the tornado center and the barometric pressure.

At 5 miles the velocity is 30 mph. Therefore

$$Vr = 5 \times 30 = 150 \text{ miles}^2/\text{hr}$$

Thus at ½-mile radius, the velocity is given by

$$\tfrac{1}{2}V = 150$$

or

$$V = 300 \text{ mph}$$

At 5 miles the pressure is 29 in. mercury, or

$$^{29}\!/_{12} \times 13.55 \times 62.4 = 2,040 \text{ psf}$$

Applying the aerodynamic form of Bernoulli's equation between the two points,

$$2,040 + \tfrac{1}{2} \times 0.00238(30 \times {}^{88}\!/_{60})^2 = p_2 + \tfrac{1}{2} \times 0.00238(300 \times {}^{88}\!/_{60})^2$$

Therefore $\qquad\qquad\qquad\qquad p_2 = 1,808 \text{ psf}$

$$= 25.62 \text{ in. mercury}$$

PROBLEMS

3·1 Two pipes of 3- and 2-in. diameter, carrying flows of velocity 50 and 25 fps respectively, flow into one 6-in.-diameter pipe. What is the velocity of flow in the large pipe?

3·2   3,000 lb/sec of water flows in a channel 30 ft wide and 18 in. deep. What is the flow velocity?

3·3   The maximum pressure available in a certain water main is 40 psia. What is the maximum pressure available at a faucet 35 ft above the main?

3·4   Calculate the pressure and velocity of the flow in the 3-in.-diameter pipe.

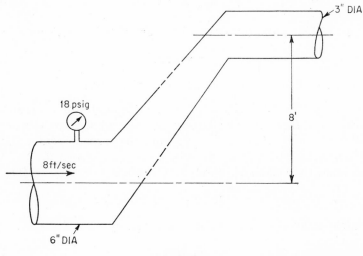

Prob. 3·4

3·5   An automatic boat bailer consists of a venturi tube drawn through the water at a speed of 10 fps, from the throat of which a tube is connected to the bottom of the boat. The maximum height that the water in the boat must be raised is 2 ft. Calculate the necessary minimum area ratio for the venturi tube.

3·6   Calculate the flow rate of water through this nozzle.

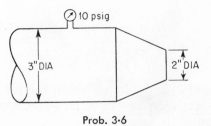

Prob. 3·6

3·7   Calculate the water flow rate through this elbow.

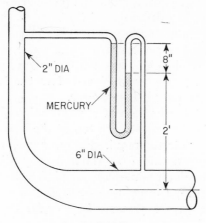

Prob. 3·7

3·8   Calculate the water flow rate from this tank.

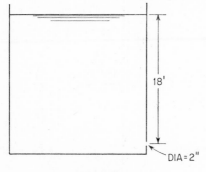

Prob. 3·8

3·9   Calculate the flow rate through this submerged orifice.

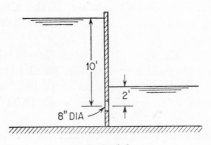

Prob. 3·9

3·10 The inlets to a submarine's buoyancy tanks are 10 ft below the surface. As the submarine sinks, the pressure difference across the inlets remains 10 ft of salt water. If the area of the inlet ports is 2 ft², how long will it take to admit 10,000 lb of seawater to the tanks?

3·11 A dam contains a head of 60 ft of water. In the base of the dam a 2-ft-diameter channel leads the water through a turbine and discharges it in air. The pressure just before the turbine is 18 psig. Calculate the turbine output horsepower.

3·12 A pump at the bottom of a 200-ft mine shaft has to pump 3 cfs of water from the base to the top of the shaft through a 3-in.-diameter pipe. Calculate the required pump horsepower.

3·13 A pump draws 0.5 cfs of water from a 4-in.-diameter main and delivers it through an 8-in.-diameter pipe. Upstream of the pump the pressure is 20 psig; at a point downstream from the pump and 10 ft vertically above it, the pressure is 28 psig. Calculate the pump horsepower.

3·14 Calculate the horsepower output of this water turbine.

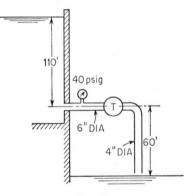

Prob. 3·14

3·15 At a point on the upper surface of an airplane wing, the air velocity is 380 mph relative to the wing. If the airplane is traveling at 300 mph at sea level ($\rho = 0.00238$ slug/ft³), what is the suction pressure at this point?

3·16 Atmospheric air ($p = 14.7$ psia, $\rho = 0.00238$ slug/ft³) is drawn through an automobile carburetor. At the throat the velocity of the air is 85 fps. Calculate the maximum height from which the suction pressure can draw gasoline ($\gamma = 42$ lb/ft³) from the float chamber.

3·17 What is the drag force due to air resistance of an automobile with an effective frontal area of 18 ft² at speeds of 30, 60, and 90 mph?

3·18 Find the terminal velocity of a 170-lb parachutist descending close to the ground with a 20-ft-diameter parachute.

3·19 Calculate the water flow rate through this vertical venturi tube. (C_v for the meter $= 0.8$.)

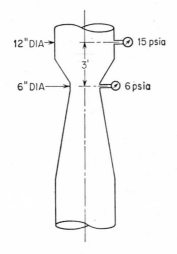

12"DIA →   15 psia

3'

6"DIA →   6 psia

Prob. 3·19

3·20 A horizontal venturi tube with an inlet diameter of 6 in. and a throat diameter of 4 in. has 3 cfs of benzine (sp gr $= 0.9$) passing through it. If the constant for the meter is 0.72, calculate the rise of mercury in an upright U-tube manometer connecting an upstream point to the throat.

3·21 An orifice meter consists of a plate with a 2-in.-diameter hole placed concentrically within a 6-in.-diameter pipe. Water flows through the pipe, causing a pressure difference of 2 ft of oil ($\gamma = 40$ lb/ft^3) across the orifice. If the constants for the meter are $C_o = 0.9$ and $C_v = 0.6$, calculate the exact flow rate and an approximate flow rate.

3·22 An orifice meter consists of a 4-in.-diameter pipe with an orifice of 3-in. diameter mounted within it. A U-tube manometer containing oil of specific weight 38 lb/ft^3 records a pressure drop of 18 in. of oil across the orifice. If the constants for the meter are $C_v = 0.7$ and $C_o = 0.82$, estimate the percentage error in using the approximate relationship to find the flow rate.

3·23 An aircraft pitot-static tube records a pressure difference of 0.6 psi at an altitude where $\rho = 0.0008$ slug/ft^3. Find the aircraft's TAS.

3·24   Find the height of the fluid in the tube.

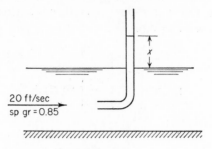

20 ft/sec
sp gr = 0.85

Prob. 3·24

3·25   18 ft from the center of a whirlpool the velocity of the water is 1 fps and the pressure 27 psia. If the vapor pressure of water is 30 psfa (at which pressure, cavitation occurs), what is the diameter of the hollow core of the whirlpool at this level?

Eg. 3-19

CHAPTER 4

The Flow of Compressible Fluids

In the preceding chapter the equations of motion and the behavior of incompressible fluids were examined. The study of compressible fluids is more complex since the density now becomes a variable, although the ideal fluid concept is still useful in solving many compressible flow problems.

4·1   Liquid compressibility

Although it is usual to regard liquids as incompressible, this is not exactly true since they are very slightly compressible.

The compressibility of a liquid is measured in terms of the bulk modulus K, which is defined in the usual way as stress/strain. For a fluid, the applied stress is the pressure increase Δp, and the strain is the relative change in volume $\Delta V/V$; thus

$$K = -\frac{\Delta p}{\Delta V/V} \qquad (4\cdot1)$$

The negative sign indicates a decrease in volume with an increase in pressure; and since the ratio $\Delta V/V$ is dimensionless, K has the same units as the pressure increment Δp. The value of K for water at normal temperatures and pressures is approximately 300,000 psi—not a very compressible fluid!

4·2   Some thermodynamic properties of gases

In order to deal with the extreme compressibility of gases, it is necessary to have a knowledge of certain thermodynamic properties for gases. The essential equations are ennumerated here, and constant reference will be made to them in this chapter. If the reader is not already familiar with these equations, he is referred for proofs to the references listed or to any elementary thermodynamics text.

The universal gas law. In its simplest form this may be stated as

$$pV = RT \tag{4·2}$$

where p = absolute pressure, psf
    V = volume, ft³
    T = absolute temperature (i.e., °F + 460 or °C + 273)
    R = gas constant for gas concerned

If Eq. (4·2) is applied to 1 lb of the gas, then V becomes the specific volume of the gas or $1/\gamma$ or $1/\rho g$. Substituting this in Eq. (4·2) gives

$$\frac{p}{\rho} = gRT \tag{4·3}$$

The value of R varies from gas to gas (for air, R = 53.3 ft/°R), but the product of R and the molecular weight of the gas is very nearly constant for all gases. This product is called the universal gas constant

$$mR = G = 1{,}550 \text{ ft/°R} \tag{4·4}$$

The isothermal process. An isothermal process is one in which the temperature remains constant. For this to occur, heat exchange between the gas and its surroundings must take place.

Equation (4·2), when applied to an isothermal process, becomes

$$pV = \text{const}$$

or

$$\frac{p}{\rho} = \text{const} \tag{4·5}$$

The adiabatic process. An adiabatic process is one in which no heat transfer occurs between the gas and its surroundings. This usually means that the process must be rapid.

If an ideal adiabatic process takes place, that is, with no friction losses, it is called an isentropic (or constant entropy) process.

Adiabatic processes obey the law

$$pV^k = \text{const}$$

or

$$\frac{p}{\rho^k} = \text{const} \tag{4·6}$$

where k is the ratio of the specific heat of the gas at constant pressure to the specific heat at constant volume, C_p/C_v. The value of k for air is 1.4.

The speed of sound. The speed of sound c is an important parameter in compressible gas flow. It may be written as

$$c^2 = \frac{kp}{\rho}$$

or since $p/\rho = gRT$,

$$c = \sqrt{kgRT} \qquad (4\cdot7)$$

Thus it can be seen that for a given gas, the acoustic velocity is proportional to the square root of the absolute temperature and independent of pressure and density.

4·3 The compressible form of Bernoulli's equation

In Art. 3·6 Bernoulli's equation for incompressible ideal flow was established from

$$\frac{dp}{\gamma} + \frac{v\,dv}{g} + dz = 0 \qquad (3\cdot4)$$

assuming γ to be constant. The compressible form may be established from the same root, remembering that γ is now a variable.

Integrating Eq. (3·4) between limits gives

$$\int_1^2 \frac{dp}{\gamma} = \int_2^1 \frac{v\,dv}{g} + \int_2^1 dz$$

$$= \frac{v_2{}^2 - v_1{}^2}{2g} + (z_2 - z_1) \qquad (4\cdot8)$$

Now it is usual when dealing with compressible gas flow problems to assume that all processes are rapid and therefore adiabatic. Thus from Eq. (4·6)

$$\frac{p}{\gamma^k} = c \qquad \text{a constant}$$

or

$$p = c\gamma^k$$

and so

$$dp = ck\gamma^{k-1}\,d\gamma$$

Substituting these in Eq. (4·8),

$$\frac{v_2{}^2 - v_1{}^2}{2g} + (z_2 - z_1) = \int_1^2 \frac{ck\gamma^{k-1}\,d\gamma}{\gamma}$$

$$= \int_1^2 ck\gamma^{k-2}\,d\gamma$$

$$= \frac{ck}{k-1}\,(\gamma_1{}^{k-1} - \gamma_2{}^{k-1})$$

$$= \frac{k}{k-1}\,c\gamma_2{}^{k-1}\left[\left(\frac{\gamma_1}{\gamma_2}\right)^{k-1} - 1\right]$$

But $\qquad\qquad\qquad c\gamma_2{}^{k-1} = c\,\dfrac{\gamma_2{}^k}{\gamma_2} = \dfrac{p_2}{\gamma_2}$

Therefore $\quad \dfrac{v_2{}^2 - v_1{}^2}{2g} + (z_2 - z_1) = \dfrac{p_2 k}{\gamma_2(k-1)}\left[\left(\dfrac{\gamma_1}{\gamma_2}\right)^{k-1} - 1\right]$

Very often in problems involving the use of this equation, the term $(z_2 - z_1)$ is negligible, in which case

$$\frac{v_2{}^2 - v_1{}^2}{2g} = \frac{p_2 k}{\gamma_2(k-1)}\left[\left(\frac{\gamma_1}{\gamma_2}\right)^{k-1} - 1\right] \qquad\qquad \textbf{(4·9)}$$

This is one form of Bernoulli's equation for ideal compressible flow. There are many other ways of writing Eq. (4·9) involving different parameters, but the student should remember that these are only alternative forms of the same equation, and not new equations. For instance, by making the substitution

$$\frac{\gamma_1}{\gamma_2} = \left(\frac{p_1}{p_2}\right)^{1/k}$$

Eq. (4·9) can be written as

$$\frac{v_2{}^2 - v_1{}^2}{2g} = \frac{p_2}{\gamma_2}\frac{k}{k-1}\left[\left(\frac{p_1}{p_2}\right)^{(k-1)/k} - 1\right] \qquad\qquad \textbf{(4·10)}$$

Or, by considering the relationship

$$\frac{\gamma_2}{\gamma_1} = \frac{p_2 T_1}{p_1 T_2} = \left(\frac{p_2}{p_1}\right)^{1/k}$$

and dividing by p_2/p_1,

$$\frac{T_1}{T_2} = \left(\frac{p_2}{p_1}\right)^{1/k-1} = \left(\frac{p_2}{p_1}\right)^{(1-k)/k} = \left(\frac{p_1}{p_2}\right)^{(k-1)/k}$$

Eq. (4·10) is reduced to

$$\frac{v_2{}^2 - v_1{}^2}{2g} = \frac{p_2}{\gamma_2} \frac{k}{k-1} \left(\frac{T_1}{T_2} - 1\right)$$

$$= RT_2 \frac{k}{k-1} \left(\frac{T_1}{T_2} - 1\right)$$

$$= \frac{Rk}{k-1} (T_1 - T_2) \qquad (4·11)$$

which is the simplest form of Bernoulli's equation.

Example 1: At one point in an air duct the temperature of the flow is 200°F and the local pressure is 30 psia. At this point the cross-sectional area of the duct is 1 ft². Downstream of this point the flow temperature is 30°F at a point where the pressure is 15 psia and the area of flow is 0.3 ft². Calculate the velocity of flow at the second point and the mass flow rate.

$$\gamma_1 = \frac{p_1}{RT_1} = \frac{30 \times 144}{53.3 \times 660} = 0.1225 \text{ lb/ft}^3$$

and

$$\gamma_2 = \frac{p_2}{RT_2} = \frac{15 \times 144}{53.3 \times 490} = 0.0825 \text{ lb/ft}^3$$

Now

$$G = \frac{\gamma_1 A_1 v_1}{g} = \frac{\gamma_2 A_2 v_2}{g}$$

Therefore

$$v_1 = \frac{\gamma_2 A_2 v_2}{\gamma_1 A_1} = \frac{0.0825}{0.1225} \times 0.3 v_2 = 0.202 v_2$$

Applying Eq. (4·11),

$$\frac{v_2{}^2 - v_1{}^2}{2g} = \frac{Rk}{k-1} (T_1 - T_2)$$

we obtain

$$\frac{v_2{}^2}{2g} (1 - 0.202^2) = \frac{53.3 \times 1.4 \times 170}{0.4}$$

so

$$v_2 = \sqrt{64.4 \times 33{,}100} = 1{,}460 \text{ fps}$$

Hence the mass flow rate is

$$\frac{\gamma_2 A_2 v_2}{g} = \frac{0.0825 \times 0.3 \times 1{,}460}{32.2} = 1.13 \text{ slugs/sec}$$

Example 2: Air is contained in a large reservoir at 25 psia and 60°F.

It exhausts to atmosphere through a convergent nozzle with an exit area of 0.5 ft². Calculate the mass flow rate.

Referring to the reservoir conditions as station 2 and the nozzle exit as station 1,

$$\gamma_2 = \frac{p_2}{RT_2} = \frac{25 \times 144}{53.3 \times 520} = 0.130 \text{ lb/ft}^3$$

Using Eq. (4·10),

$$\frac{0 - v_1^2}{2g} = \frac{25 \times 144 \times 1.4}{0.130 \times 0.4} \left[\left(\frac{14.7}{25} \right)^{0.4/1.4} - 1 \right]$$

$$= 9.7 \times 10^4 \left[\left(\frac{14.7}{25} \right)^{0.286} - 1 \right]$$

Therefore $v_1^2 = 6.24 \times 10^6 (1 - 0.859) = 6.24 \times 0.141 \times 10^6$

hence $v_1 = 940$ fps

Now $\dfrac{\gamma_1}{\gamma_2} = \left(\dfrac{p_1}{p_2} \right)^{1/k}$

so $\gamma_1 = \gamma_2 \left(\dfrac{p_1}{p_2} \right)^{1/k} = 0.130 \left(\dfrac{14.7}{25} \right)^{0.715} = 0.089 \text{ lb/ft}^3$

Therefore $G = \rho_1 A_1 v_1 = \dfrac{0.089 \times 940 \times 0.5}{32.2} = 1.30 \text{ slugs/sec}$

4·4   Mach number

The four basic equations with which all compressible flow problems may be solved have now been established. These are:
1. *The universal gas law,* $p/\gamma = RT$
2. *The adiabatic law,* $p/\gamma^k = $ const
3. *The equation of continuity,* $\rho A v = $ const
4. *Bernoulli's equation in its various forms*

A new parameter which will help in the study of compressible flows is now introduced. This is the ratio of local velocity to local acoustic velocity, called the *mach number* (after the Austrian physicist Ernst Mach) and given the symbol M.

For subsonic flows M is less than 1, and for supersonic flows M is greater than 1. The region in which M approximately equals 1 is called the transonic region.

Example: Calculate the exit mach number for the nozzle of Example 2, Art. 4·3.

At the nozzle the speed of sound is given by

$$c^2 = \frac{kpg}{\rho}$$

$$= \frac{1.4 \times 14.7 \times 144 \times 32.2}{0.089}$$

Therefore $c = 1{,}036$ fps

Hence $M = \dfrac{v}{c} = \dfrac{940}{1{,}036} = 0.907$

(speed of Sound)

4.5   Stagnation pressure in subsonic compressible flow   *→ M = less than 1*

Consider the flow along the streamline shown in Fig. 4·1. O is a point in the undisturbed free stream, and S is a stagnation point. The flow is everywhere subsonic.

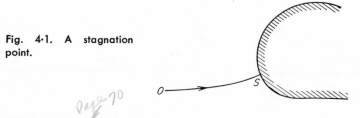

Fig. 4·1.   A   stagnation point.

page 70

Applying Eq. (4·10) to this flow,

$$\frac{V_0{}^2}{2g} = \frac{p_0 k}{\gamma_0(k-1)}\left[\left(\frac{p_s}{p_0}\right)^{(k-1)/k} - 1\right]$$

since $V_s = 0$. Rearranging for p_s,

$$p_s = p_0\left(1 + \frac{V_0{}^2\gamma_0(k-1)}{2gp_0 k}\right)^{k/(k-1)}$$

Now for convenience writing

$$\frac{V_0{}^2\gamma_0}{gp_0} = Z$$

$$p_s = p_0\left(1 + \frac{Z}{2}\frac{k-1}{k}\right)^{k/(k-1)}$$

Expanding this binomially,

$$p_s = p_0 \left(1 + \frac{Z}{2} + \frac{Z^2}{8k} + \cdots \right)$$

$$= p_0 + \frac{Zp_0}{2} \left(1 + \frac{Z}{4k} + \cdots \right)$$

Now
$$\frac{Z}{k} = \frac{V_0{}^2 \gamma_0}{kp_0 g} = \frac{V_0{}^2}{c^2} = M^2$$

and
$$\frac{Z}{2} p_0 = \frac{1}{2} \frac{V_0{}^2 \gamma_0}{g} = \frac{1}{2} \rho_0 V_0{}^2$$

Therefore
$$p_s = p_0 + \tfrac{1}{2}\rho_0 V_0{}^2 \left(1 + \frac{M^2}{4} + \cdots \right) \tag{4.12}$$

It will be noticed that the compressible stagnation pressure is higher than the incompressible stagnation pressure by an amount proportional to the term in the bracket, referred to as the *mach factor MF*. This means that a pitot-static tube designed to read velocities in incompressible flow will read high if used in a compressible flow without correction.

The error involved in neglecting terms in the mach factor becomes greater as M approaches unity, and at mach numbers greater than unity the equation is no longer valid because of the existence of shock waves (see Art. 4.6) ahead of the stagnation point.

Example: An ASI is calibrated for incompressible flow. Calculate the pilot's observed speed if the TAS is 480 mph at (*a*) sea level, and (*b*) 25,000 ft.

(*a*) At sea level, $\rho = 0.00238$ slug/ft³, $T = 60°F$. Therefore

$$c = \sqrt{kgRT} = \sqrt{1.4 \times 32.2 \times 53.3 \times 520} = 1{,}120 \text{ fps}$$

Hence
$$M = \frac{V}{c} = \frac{480 \times 88}{1{,}120 \times 60} = 0.622$$

and so
$$\frac{M^2}{4} = 0.0967$$

Therefore
$$p_s - p_0 = \tfrac{1}{2}\rho_0 V_0{}^2 (1.0967)$$

neglecting terms in M^4, etc. Now since the instrument is calibrated for incompressible flow, it reads this as $\rho_0 V_i{}^2/2$, where V_i is the indicated velocity and ρ_0 is the sea-level value of the density.

Therefore
$$V_i{}^2 = V_0{}^2 \times 1.0967$$
or
$$V_i = 480 \sqrt{1.0967} = 502 \text{ mph}$$

(b) At 25,000 ft, $\rho = 0.00107$ slug/ft³, $T = -30°F$. At this height, then,

$$c = 1,120 \sqrt{430/520} = 1,020 \text{ fps}$$

Hence

$$M = \frac{480 \times 88}{1,020 \times 60} = 0.682$$

and so

$$\frac{M^2}{4} = 0.116$$

Therefore

$$p_s - p_0 = \tfrac{1}{2}\rho V_0^2 \times 1.116$$

Again the instrument reads this as $\tfrac{1}{2}\rho_0 V_i^2$; therefore

$$V_i^2 = \frac{\rho}{\rho_0} V_0^2 \times 1.116$$

or

$$V_i = V_0 \sqrt{1.116 \frac{\rho}{\rho_0}}$$

$$= 480 \sqrt{1.116 \frac{0.00107}{0.00238}} = 341 \text{ mph}$$

4·6 Shock waves

When a supersonic flow is retarded sufficiently, a shock wave occurs in the flow, across which the *normal* velocity component changes from supersonic to subsonic abruptly. At the same time the fluid density, pressure, and temperature all rise suddenly across the shock wave.

The strength of the shock wave depends upon the initial mach number, high mach numbers producing stronger shock waves than low mach numbers. The shock wave itself is a thin region of fluid in which large entropy increases occur with considerable friction, and thus it cannot be considered an isentropic process. This means that *some* of the previously derived equations do not apply across a shock wave.

The universal gas law and the equation of continuity hold across a shock wave, but neither Bernoulli's equation nor the adiabatic gas law may be applied.

The theory of shock waves is beyond the scope of this text; however, the following results for a normal shock wave (that is, a shock wave perpendicular to the flow direction) are quoted without proof. The reader is referred to the selected references for proofs when required.

The mach number behind a normal shock is related to the mach number ahead of the shock by the equation

$$M_2 = \left(\frac{1 + [(k-1)/2]M_1^2}{kM_1^2 - (k-1)/2} \right)^{1/2} \tag{4·13}$$

The pressure ratio across a normal shock is given by

$$\frac{p_2}{p_1} = \frac{1 + kM_1^2}{1 + kM_2^2} \qquad (4\cdot14)$$

and the temperature ratio by

$$\frac{T_1}{T_2} = \frac{1 + [(k-1)/2]M_2^2}{1 + [(k-1)/2]M_1^2} \qquad (4\cdot15)$$

Example: The flow of air in the working section of a Mach 3 supersonic wind tunnel is decelerated by means of a normal shock. If the working section has a temperature of 300°R and the pressure behind the shock is atmospheric, calculate the pressure and velocity in the working section and the mach number and velocity behind the shock.

In the working section

$$c_1 = \sqrt{1.4 \times 32.2 \times 53.3 \times 300} = 850 \text{ fps}$$

Therefore $\quad v_1 = 3c_1 = 2{,}550 \text{ fps}$

Behind the shock

$$M_2 = \left(\frac{1 + 0.2 \times 9}{1.4 \times 9 - 0.2}\right)^{1/2} = 0.475$$

and

$$p_2 = p_1\left(\frac{1 + 1.4 \times 9}{1 + 1.4 \times 0.225}\right)$$

Therefore

$$p_1 = 14.7\,\frac{1.315}{13.6} = 1.42 \text{ psia}$$

The temperature behind the shock is given by

$$T_2 = 300\,\frac{1 + 0.2 \times 9}{1 + 0.2 \times 0.225} = 808°\text{R}$$

Therefore $\quad c_2 = \sqrt{1.4 \times 32.2 \times 53.3 \times 808} = 1{,}395 \text{ fps}$

so $\quad v_2 = M_2 c_2 = 0.475 \times 1{,}395 = 662 \text{ fps}$

4·7 The rate of change of area with mach number

The equation of continuity states that

$$G = \rho A V$$

Taking logarithms of this,

$$\ln G = \ln \rho + \ln A + \ln V$$

and differentiating,

$$0 = \frac{d\rho}{\rho} + \frac{dA}{A} + \frac{dV}{V}$$

Now Eq. (3·4) states that

$$\frac{dp}{\gamma} = -\frac{V\,dV}{g}$$

if terms in dz are neglected, or

$$\frac{dp}{\rho} = -V\,dV$$

The adiabatic gas law may be written as

$$\rho = cp^{1/k}$$

and differentiating,

$$d\rho = \frac{c}{k}\,p^{1/k-1}\,dp = \frac{\rho}{kp}\,dp = \frac{dp}{c^2}$$

Therefore

$$\frac{d\rho}{\rho} = \frac{1}{c^2}\frac{dp}{\rho} = -\frac{V\,dV}{c^2}$$

and so

$$\frac{dA}{A} = -\frac{d\rho}{\rho} - \frac{dV}{V} = \frac{V\,dV}{c^2} - \frac{dV}{V}$$

$$= \frac{dV}{V}\,(M^2 - 1) \tag{4·16}$$

It will be immediately noticed that at sonic velocity $(M = 1)$ the sign of dA/dV changes. In other words, subsonically the velocity of the flow increases with a decrease in flow area, until sonic velocity occurs. If the flow is to accelerate further, the area of the duct must *increase* downstream of the point where sonic velocity occurs.

Naturally this process may not be continued indefinitely, the limiting mach number depending on the pressure ratio. If the back pressure is too high, the flow will revert to subsonic by means of a shock wave, thus restoring the pressure to the required value.

4·8 The critical pressure ratio

Consider the ideal frictionless flow from a very large reservoir through the entirely convergent nozzle shown in Fig. 4·2. The discharge takes place into a region of pressure p_3.

Whatever happens, the pressure at the nozzle exit p_2 cannot be less than p_3; and if sonic velocity is to be achieved, it must occur at the nozzle exit.

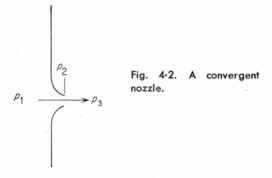

Fig. 4·2. A convergent nozzle.

Applying Eq. (4·10) between the reservoir and the nozzle exit,

$$\frac{V_2{}^2}{2g} = \frac{p_2 k}{\gamma_2 (k-1)} \left[\left(\frac{p_1}{p_2} \right)^{(k-1)/k} - 1 \right]$$

since $V_1 = 0$. Now replacing $V_2{}^2$ by $c_2{}^2 = k p_2 g / \gamma_2$ and substituting $(p_1/p_2)_{\text{crit}}$ for p_1/p_2,

$$\frac{k p_2}{2 \gamma_2} = \frac{p_2 k}{\gamma_2 (k-1)} \left[\left(\frac{p_1}{p_2} \right)_{\text{crit}}^{(k-1)/k} - 1 \right]$$

or

$$\frac{k-1}{2} + 1 = \left(\frac{p_1}{p_2} \right)_{\text{crit}}^{(k-1)/k}$$

Hence

$$\left(\frac{p_1}{p_2} \right)_{\text{crit}} = \left(\frac{k+1}{2} \right)^{k/(k-1)}$$

or more usually

$$\left(\frac{p_2}{p_1} \right)_{\text{crit}} = \left(\frac{2}{k+1} \right)^{k/(k-1)} \qquad (4·17)$$

If the ratio p_3/p_1 is equal to this critical pressure ratio, sonic velocity will occur at the nozzle exit, and the nozzle exit pressure p_2 will equal p_3. If the value of p_3/p_1 is less than the required critical ratio, sonic velocity will still occur at the nozzle exit, but the pressure p_2 will be greater than p_3, and further expansion will take place *outside the nozzle*.

If the ratio p_3/p_1 is greater than the critical ratio, sonic velocity will not occur, and again p_2 and p_3 will be equal.

The value of the critical ratio for air is 0.528.

Example: Air flows from a reservoir at 30 psia and 520°R through a convergent nozzle with an exit area of 0.5 in.² into atmospheric pressure. Calculate the nozzle exit temperature and the mass flow rate.

$$\frac{p_3}{p_1} = \frac{14.7}{30} = 0.49 \qquad <0.528$$

and so sonic velocity will occur at the exit. The nozzle pressure is then

$$p_2 = 0.528 \times 30 = 15.85 \text{ psia}$$

In the reservoir

$$\gamma_1 = \frac{p_1}{RT_1} = \frac{30 \times 144}{53.3 \times 520} = 0.155 \text{ lb/ft}^3$$

and

$$\frac{p_1}{\gamma_1{}^k} = \frac{p_2}{\gamma_2{}^k}$$

So

$$\gamma_2 = \gamma_1 \left(\frac{p_2}{p_1}\right)^{1/k} = 0.155(0.528)^{0.714}$$

$$= 0.0984 \text{ lb/ft}^3$$

At the nozzle

$$T_2 = \frac{p_2}{R\gamma_2} = \frac{15.85 \times 144}{0.0984 \times 53.3} = 435°R$$

and so

$$V_2 = c_2 = \sqrt{1.4 \times 32.2 \times 53.3 \times 435}$$

$$= 1,022 \text{ fps}$$

Therefore

$$G = \gamma A V = 0.0984 \times \frac{0.5}{144} \times 1,022$$

$$= 0.35 \text{ lb/sec}$$

4·9 The convergent-divergent nozzle

If it is desired to cause the exit flow from a nozzle to be supersonic, as might be the case in a rocket exhaust for instance, then it is necessary to use a convergent-divergent nozzle as shown in Fig. 4·3.

Fig. 4·3. A convergent-divergent nozzle.

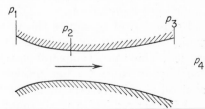

The flow accelerates subsonically in the convergent section, reaching Mach 1 at the throat, in which case the ratio p_2/p_1 is the critical ratio for the gas concerned.

Supersonic acceleration takes place in the divergent section, provided that the ratio p_4/p_1 is sufficiently small.

The convergent section can be fairly short, but the divergent section is usually comparatively long in order to prevent flow breakaway from the walls.

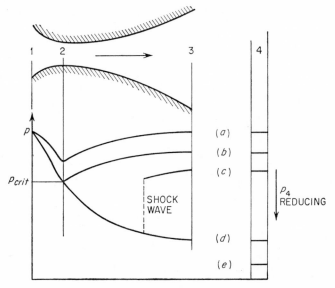

Fig. 4·4.   Pressure variations through a convergent-divergent nozzle.

Figure 4·4 shows the variations in pressure through a convergent-divergent nozzle. Of course the important parameter in convergent-divergent nozzle problems is the ratio p_4/p_1; but in order to clarify the explanation, p_1 is assumed to be constant and p_4 is allowed to fall in stages.

Curve a shows an entirely subsonic flow case. The velocity at the throat is subsonic, the pressure at the throat is greater than the critical value, and p_3 equals p_4.

Reduction of p_4 causes the velocity at the throat to increase until sonic velocity occurs. p_2/p_1 is now the critical ratio for the gas concerned. This case is shown in curve b. However the back pressure p_4 is too high to cause further acceleration, and the flow decelerates subsonically in the divergent section to make p_3 equal p_4 again.

A further reduction of p_4 cannot affect the flow before the throat, but causes the flow to accelerate supersonically after it. If the reduction in p_4 is fairly small, as shown in the case of curve c, it is not sufficient to maintain continuous acceleration to the exit. In this case a normal shock occurs in the supersonic flow and causes the velocity to become subsonic with a corresponding pressure increase. Deceleration will now occur in the remainder of the divergent section. Again p_3 equals p_4.

If p_4 is now reduced sufficiently, full expansion will occur. In this state acceleration takes place throughout the divergent section so that p_3 equals p_4. This is shown in Fig. 4·4d.

If p_4 is reduced below this full expansion level, no difference in flow is observed in the nozzle, and the pressures remain as shown in (d). However, since p_3 is greater than p_4, further expansion will take place outside the nozzle.

Example: The products of combustion of a small rocket engine pass through a frictionless convergent-divergent nozzle with a throat area of 1 in.². In the combustion chamber, the pressure is 100 psia and the temperature is 800°R. The values of k and R are 1.3 and 41 ft/°R respectively. If the back pressure is 14.7 psia, calculate the conditions at the throat, the exit mach number, and the exit area required for full expansion.

In the chamber

$$\gamma_1 = \frac{p_1}{RT_1} = \frac{100 \times 144}{41 \times 800} = 0.439 \text{ lb/ft}^3$$

At the throat

$$\left(\frac{p_2}{p_1}\right)_{\text{crit}} = \left(\frac{2}{k+1}\right)^{k/(k-1)} = 0.546$$

Therefore $\qquad p_2 = 54.6$ psia

and $\qquad \gamma_2 = \gamma_1 \left(\frac{p_2}{p_1}\right)^{1/k} = 0.439(0.546)^{0.77}$

$$= 0.276 \text{ lb/ft}^3$$

For sonic velocity at the throat

$$v_2 = c_2 = \sqrt{\frac{kgp}{\gamma}} = 1{,}192 \text{ fps}$$

Hence the weight flow rate is

$$A_2\gamma_2 V_2 = \frac{0.276 \times 1{,}192}{144} = 2.28 \text{ lb/sec}$$

At exit, for full expansion, $p_3 = p_4$. Therefore

$$\gamma_3 = \gamma_1 \left(\frac{p_3}{p_1}\right)^{1/k} = 0.100 \text{ lb/ft}^3$$

and so
$$T_3 = \frac{p_3}{R\gamma_3} = \frac{14.7 \times 144}{41.0 \times 0.1} = 516°R$$

Now since $V_1^2 \doteq 0$,

$$\frac{V_3^2}{2g} = \frac{Rk}{k-1}(T_1 - T_3)$$

or
$$V_3 = \sqrt{\frac{2gRk}{k-1}(T_1 - T_3)} = 1,805 \text{ fps}$$

and
$$c_3 = \sqrt{kgRT_3} = 942 \text{ fps}$$

Therefore
$$M_3 = \frac{V_3}{c_3} = 1.92$$

For full expansion

$$2.28 = \gamma_3 A_3 V_3 = 0.1A_3 \times 1,805$$

or
$$A_3 = 0.0126 \text{ ft}^2 = 1.82 \text{ in.}^2$$

PROBLEMS

4·1 An applied pressure of 6,000 psi is found to reduce the volume of a certain liquid from 1 to 0.98 ft³. Calculate the bulk modulus of the fluid.

4·2 Seawater at the surface has a specific weight of 64.0 lb/ft³ and a bulk modulus of 3×10^5 psi. Calculate the specific weight of seawater at a depth where the pressure is 3,100 psi.

4·3 What is the temperature of a mass of air with a specific weight of 0.10 lb/ft³ when the pressure is 120 psia?

4·4 Standard air is considered to have a pressure of 14.7 psia, a temperature of 58°F, and a density of 0.00238 slug/ft³. Estimate the value of R.

4·5 The air of Prob. 4·4 is compressed isothermally to a pressure of 100 psia. Calculate its new specific weight.

4·6 Air at 100°F and 15 psia is compressed adiabatically to 60 psia. Calculate the specific weight before and after the compression.

4·7 Air from a service station storage tank at 100 psia and 60°F is used to inflate a tire to 30 psig. Assuming adiabatic expansion, calculate the temperature of the air entering the tire at 30 psig.

4·8   Carbon dioxide at 32°F and 14.7 psia is compressed until its density is 0.0085 slug/ft³. What are the pressure and temperature of the gas at this point?

4·9   An automobile with a compression ratio of 8:1 draws in air at 14.7 psia and 60°F. What are the temperature, pressure, and specific weight of the air at top dead center? (Neglect the effects due to gasoline.)

4·10   Calculate the speed of sound in air at 20 psig when the density is 0.004 slugs/ft³.

4·11   Calculate the speed of sound in air and carbon dioxide at 60°F.

4·12   What is the speed of an aircraft traveling at $M = 2.5$ at an altitude of 40,000 ft?

4·13   Carbon dioxide flows from a reservoir, where the pressure is 60 psia and the temperature 70°F, through a 4-in.-diameter pipe in which the pressure is measured as 35 psia. Calculate the mass flow rate, the temperature, and the mach number in the pipe.

4·14   Air is flowing in a divergent duct. At a point where the duct diameter is 3 in., the pressure and temperature are 75 psia and 750°F. Farther along the pipe, at a point where the diameter is 4 in., the pressure is 15 psia. Calculate the mass flow rate and the velocity and mach number at each point.

4·15   Air flows through a pipe of 4.4-in. diameter with a velocity of 1,370 fps. The pipe diameter increases to 6 in., and the velocity of flow is seen to increase to 2,650 fps. Calculate the mach number in the large-diameter pipe.

4·16   Deduce the next term in the expression for the mach factor

$$\left(1 + \frac{M^2}{4} + \cdots\right)$$

4·17   Calculate the pressure on the nose of an object in an airstream of Mach 0.8 at a temperature of 400°F when the airstream static pressure is 8 in. of mercury absolute.

4·18   A normal shock occurs in an airstream of Mach 2.8. Calculate the mach number behind the shock.

4·19   If the pressure upstream of the shock of Prob. 4·18 is 1.66 psia, calculate the pressure downstream of the shock.

4·20   If the pressure and temperature of the flow of Prob. 4·18 are 300°F and 1.66 psia, calculate the stagnation pressure of the flow.

4·21   Show that the density ratio across a normal shock is given by

$$\frac{\rho_2}{\rho_1} = \frac{[(k + 1)/2]M_1^2}{1 + [(k - 1)/2]M_1^2}$$

4·22   Calculate the critical pressure ratio for carbon dioxide.

4·23   A tank containing nitrogen at 60°F discharges into atmosphere ($p = 14.7$ psia) through a convergent nozzle with a 1-in.-diameter exit. Calculate the minimum tank pressure that will cause the flow to be sonic at exit and the mass flow under these conditions.

4·24   Air flows through a convergent-divergent nozzle from atmosphere ($p = 14.7$ psia, $T = 60°F$) into a tank in which the pressure is maintained at 20 in. of mercury vacuum. Calculate the mach number at exit, assuming full expansion.

4·25   Air flows from a reservoir, in which the pressure and temperature are 60 psia and 200°F, through a convergent-divergent nozzle of 2-in. throat diameter into a region of 14.7 psia pressure. Calculate the diameter of the exit for full expansion.

CHAPTER 5

Fluid Impulse and Jet Propulsion

5·1 The principle of momentum

Momentum is defined as the product of the mass and the velocity of a body and is a measure of the energy of motion stored in a moving object. It is a vector quantity in that it has direction as well as magnitude. A change in momentum can only be produced by the application of an external force, and therefore a change in momentum implies the application of such a force. The last statement is the principle of momentum and may be demonstrated as follows.

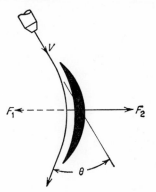

Fig. 5·1. Fluid deflected by a stationary blade.

In Fig. 5·1 the nozzle ejects a steady stream of fluid at a velocity V. The stream of fluid strikes a stationary blade and is deflected through an angle θ, causing the fluid momentum to change direction (but not magnitude in this case as friction is ignored). To cause this change in momentum, a force F_1 has been exerted by the blade on the fluid, and a reaction force F_2 exactly equal and opposite to F_1 has been exerted by the fluid on the blade. This reaction force can be used to cause the blade to move and do work.

5·2 The impulse-momentum equation

The impulse-momentum equation is used to calculate the forces exerted on a solid boundary by a moving fluid stream. It can readily be derived from the familiar Newtonian relation, $F = Ma$.

Force = Mass × acceleration

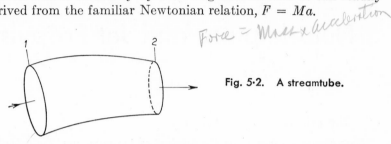

Fig. 5·2. A streamtube.

Consider the flow through the streamtube shown in Fig. 5·2. The fluid at section 1 reaches section 2 in a finite time Δt. If the flow rate through the streamtube is Q cfs, then the *mass* flowing between sections 1 and 2 is

flow rate   time

$$Q\, \Delta t\, \rho \qquad \text{density}$$

and the equation of motion becomes

Force
$$\mathbf{F} = Q\, \Delta t\, \rho \times \text{acceleration}$$

(Note that **F** is considered a vector force.)

Now the acceleration is given by

$$\frac{\Delta \mathbf{V}}{\Delta t}$$

and therefore

$$\mathbf{F} = Q\, \Delta t\, \rho\, \frac{\Delta \mathbf{V}}{\Delta t} = Q\rho\, \Delta \mathbf{V} \qquad (5\cdot1)$$

change of velocity

since Δt is a finite time interval.

Also, $\Delta \mathbf{V}$ is the vector change in velocity and equals

$$\mathbf{V}_2 - \mathbf{V}_1$$

Hence Eq. (5·1) can be written in its final vector form,

$$\mathbf{F} = Q\rho(\mathbf{V}_2 - \mathbf{V}_1) \qquad (5\cdot2)$$

Vector change

This is called the general impulse-momentum equation and stated in words means that *the force required to produce a change of momentum in a fluid is equal to the rate of change of fluid momentum.*

5·3   Application of the impulse-momentum equation

In the preceding article the impulse-momentum equation was derived by considering the flow through a streamtube. Since the definition of a streamtube shows it to have no flow across its walls, the tube can be considered a solid boundary, and the flow through pipes may thus be dealt with directly.

The fluid flowing through the combination bend and contraction shown in Fig. 5·3 has its direction changed through an angle θ and its velocity changed from V_1 to V_2 as it passes from section 1 to section 2.

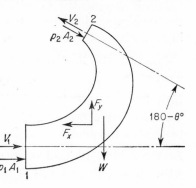

Fig. 5·3. A combined bend and contraction.

The forces acting *on the fluid* are:

1. The pressure forces p_1A_1 and p_2A_2 at the entry and exit respectively
2. The weight of the fluid contained in the bend
3. A complex of pressure forces at the sides of the bend, summarized as the horizontal and vertical forces F_x and F_y

The resultant R of F_x and F_y is the force exerted on the fluid by the bend and is exactly equal and opposite to the force exerted on the bend by the fluid; the latter is the force usually required.

Since this problem is essentially two-dimensional, it will be sufficient to apply Eq. (5·2) in the horizontal and vertical directions.

Resolving forces in the horizontal direction and considering the positive direction to be in the direction of the flow,

$$p_1A_1 - p_2A_2 \cos \theta - F_x$$

is the horizontal accelerating force, and the horizontal velocity change is

$$V_2 \cos \theta - V_1$$

Hence, from Eq. (5·2),

$$p_1A_1 - p_2A_2 \cos \theta - F_x = Q\rho(V_2 \cos \theta - V_1) \qquad \textbf{(5·3a)}$$

Now resolving vertically,

$$F_y - W - p_2A_2 \sin \theta \; = 0$$

is the vertical accelerating force, and the vertical velocity change is

$$V_2 \sin \theta - 0$$

Hence $\qquad F_y - W - p_2A_2 \sin \theta = Q\rho(V_2 \sin \theta - 0) \qquad \textbf{(5·3b)}$

It will frequently be necessary to apply Bernoulli's equation to determine one of the pressures involved. For small bends the variation in potential at the inlet and outlet may be ignored, but for bends with large vertical dimensions the potential variation must be taken into account.

With this additional information Eqs. (5·3a) and (5·3b) may be solved for F_x and F_y, both of which will be positive if their direction was correctly chosen initially. A negative value for either merely indicates that the chosen direction was initially incorrect.

Example 1: A 12-in.-diameter horizontal pipe terminates in a nozzle with an exit diameter of 3 in., as shown in Fig. 5·4. If water flows

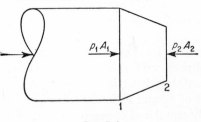

Fig. 5·4

through the pipe at a rate of 5 cfs, calculate the force exerted on the nozzle.

From symmetry, there is no F_y force. The velocities at stations 1 and 2 are given by

$$A_1V_1 = A_2V_2 = Q$$

Therefore $\qquad V_1 = \dfrac{5}{\pi/4} = 6.3$ fps

and $\qquad V_2 = 16 \times 6.3 = 102$ fps

Since the nozzle is discharging into atmosphere, $p_2 = 0$. Applying Bernoulli's equation between stations 1 and 2 to find p_1,

$$\frac{p_1}{62.4} + \frac{6.3^2}{2g} + 0 = \frac{102^2}{2g} + 0 + 0$$

since $z_1 = z_2 = 0$. Therefore

$$p_1 = \frac{102^2 - 6.3^2}{2g} \, 62.4 = 9{,}850 \text{ psfg} \quad \textit{gage pressure}$$

Now applying Eq. (5·2) in the direction of flow gives

$$p_1 A_1 - p_2 A_2 - F_x = Q\rho(V_2 - V_1)$$

or $\qquad 9{,}850 \times \dfrac{\pi}{4} - F_x = 5 \times \dfrac{62.4}{32.2}(102 - 6.3)$

Hence $\qquad\qquad F_x = 9{,}850 \times \dfrac{\pi}{4} - \dfrac{5 \times 62.4 \times 95.7}{32.2}$

$$= 6{,}820 \text{ lb}$$

Since F_x is positive, the assumed direction of F_x was correct. This is the force exerted by the nozzle on the fluid, and therefore the force exerted on the nozzle is 6,820 lb in the downstream direction.

Example 2: Water flows round a 90° vertical bend through a pipe with a diameter of 8 in., as shown in Fig. 5·5. The volume of the bend

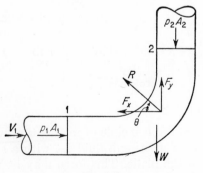

Fig. 5·5

is 1 ft³, and the exit from the bend is 1 ft above the horizontal center line. Calculate the magnitude and direction of the force on the elbow for a flow rate of 2.5 cfs if the mean pressure in the horizontal pipe is 300 psf.

Bernoulli's equation is used to calculate p_2; $V_1 = V_2$, $z_1 = 0$, and $z_2 = 1$. Therefore

$$\frac{p_2}{\gamma} + 1 = \frac{p_1}{\gamma}$$

and so $\qquad p_2 = p_1 - \gamma = 300 - 62.4 = 237.6 \text{ psf}$

Now $\qquad\qquad V = \frac{Q}{A}$

$$= \frac{2.5 \times 9}{\pi} = 7.15 \text{ fps}$$

Applying Eq. (5·2) horizontally,

$$p_1 A_1 - F_x = Q\rho(0 - V) = -Q\rho V$$

Therefore $\qquad\qquad F_x = \frac{300\pi}{9} + 2.5 \frac{62.4}{32.2} \times 7.15$

$$= 139 \text{ lb}$$

And vertically,

$$F_y - W - p_2 A_2 = Q\rho V$$

Therefore $\qquad\qquad F_y = \frac{2.5 \times 62.4 \times 7.15}{32.2} + 62.4 + 237.6\frac{\pi}{9}$

$$= 180 \text{ lb}$$

Hence the resultant force acting on the fluid (equal and opposite to the required force) is

$$\sqrt{139^2 + 180^2} = 227 \text{ lb}$$

and the angle θ is

$$\theta = \arctan {}^{180}\!/_{139} = 52.2°$$

5·4 The impulse turbine

In Arts. 5·1 and 5·2 the principle of momentum was discussed, and it was shown that by deflecting a fluid jet with a stationary blade a force was exerted on the blade. This force may be used to cause the blade to move and do work, which is the basic principle of the impulse turbine.

Naturally the force on the blade will be modified by the blade movement, and a single blade would soon move away from the influence of the fluid jet. The latter problem is overcome by providing a series of blades around the periphery of a turbine so that one or more of the blades is constantly in the jet. The force on the moving blades will be proportional to the rate of change of fluid momentum *relative to the blades*.

Consider the flow of fluid into a row of turbine blades, as shown in the end view of Fig. 5·6. The fluid enters the turbine with an absolute velocity V_1 at an absolute inlet angle of θ_1. This total velocity vector may be considered to consist of two component vectors—v, equal to and in the direction of the blade velocity, and U_1, the inlet velocity of the fluid relative to the blades. The vector U_1 controls the power output of the turbine, and the angle α_1 which it makes with the blade velocity must be the blade inlet angle if smooth entry flow is to occur.

Figure 5·7 shows the velocity diagram for the fluid leaving the turbine blades. The absolute outlet velocity V_2 may be considered to

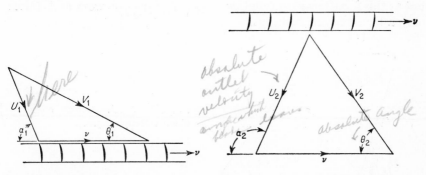

Fig. 5·6. Impulse turbine inlet velocity diagram.

Fig. 5·7. Impulse turbine exit velocity diagram.

consist of the two components v and U_2; the latter is the outlet velocity of the fluid relative to the blades. The angle α_2 which it makes with the blade direction must be the blade outlet angle, since the flow must leave the blades tangentially relative to the blades. The angle θ_2 is the absolute outlet angle of the fluid.

In the absence of friction, the velocity of the fluid relative to the blades remains constant in magnitude, although its direction is changed, so that $U_1 = U_2$. If friction is present, then U_2 will be less than U_1.

Both the previous velocity diagrams (Figs. 5·6 and 5·7) are based on a side of length v and are usually superimposed into a single combined velocity diagram based on this length, as shown in Fig. 5·8. From this diagram the turbine performance may be evaluated as follows.

The absolute change in velocity in the x direction is given by ΔV_x and may be measured from the diagram. Using Eq. (5·2) to evaluate the force required to cause this velocity change yields

$$F_x = Q\rho\,\Delta V_x$$

Since the force moves with a velocity v, the work done by the turbine is

$$P = F_x v = Q\rho\,\Delta V_x v \qquad \text{ft-lb/sec} \tag{5·4}$$

Similarly, there is an axial force F_y given by

$$F_y = Q\rho\,\Delta V_y$$

but as this force moves through no distance, it does no work and causes only a thrust at the bearings.

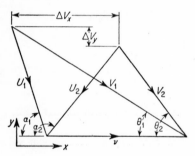

Fig. 5·8. Impulse turbine combined velocity diagram.

The power output is a maximum for any given blade speed when $\alpha_1 = 0°$ and $\alpha_2 = 180°$, since this gives the largest possible value for ΔV_x. For such a condition, the fluid must enter and leave the blades tangentially so that $\theta_1 = \theta_2 = 0°$, and it may be shown that the maximum possible output is under these conditions and when $v = V_1/2$.

Since the energy content of the fluid entering the turbine is

$$\frac{p_1}{\gamma} + \frac{V_1{}^2}{2g} + z_1 + I_1 \qquad \text{ft-lb/lb}$$

and that of the fluid leaving the turbine is

$$\frac{p_2}{\gamma} + \frac{V_2{}^2}{2g} + z_2 + I_2 \qquad \text{ft-lb/lb}$$

then the energy absorbed by the turbine is

$$\left[\left(\frac{p_1}{\gamma} + \frac{V_1{}^2}{2g} + z_1 + I_1\right) - \left(\frac{p_2}{\gamma} + \frac{V_2{}^2}{2g} + z_2 + I_2\right)\right] Q\gamma \qquad \text{ft-lb/sec}$$

and the turbine efficiency is

$$\frac{\text{hp output} \times 550}{[(p_1/\gamma + V_1{}^2/2g + z_1 + I_1) - (p_2/\gamma + V_2{}^2/2g + z_2 + I_2)]Q\gamma} = \eta \qquad (5\cdot5)$$

For liquids, when $p_1 = p_2$, $z_1 = z_2$, and $I_1 = I_2$, this reduces to

$$\eta = \frac{2 \times \text{hp} \times 550}{Q\rho(V_1{}^2 - V_2{}^2)} \qquad (5\cdot6)$$

Equation (5·4) gives the horsepower as

$$\frac{Q\rho \, \Delta V_x v}{550}$$

V_1 & V_2 absolute velocities in actual

Therefore
$$\eta = \frac{2 \, \Delta V_x v}{V_1{}^2 - V_2{}^2} \qquad (5\cdot7)$$

Example 1: 5 cfs of water flows into an impulse turbine with a velocity of 350 fps at an absolute inlet angle of 80° to the blade direction. The turbine blade velocity is 200 fps, and the efflux velocity is 250 fps. Calculate the required blade inlet and outlet angles and the horsepower output of the turbine in the absence of friction.

The turbine velocity diagram (see Fig. 5·9) can be constructed as follows:
1. Draw the base AB equal to 200 fps. (1 in. = 100 fps.)
2. From B draw V_1 at 80° to AB and 3.5 in. long. The closing side AC is now the inlet velocity relative to the blades. The magnitude of this is unchanged in passing over the blades.
3. Draw the arc CC' centered at A.
4. Since the final velocity V_2 is 250 fps, draw the arc $C'C''$ centered at B with a radius of 2.5 in. The point C' is the apex of the second velocity triangle, and so the diagram can be completed.

From these triangles the blade inlet and outlet angles α_1 and α_2 can be measured and are found to be

$$\alpha_1 = 112° \qquad \alpha_2 = 141°$$

The absolute change in velocity in the direction of the blade motion is given by ΔV_x and equals 150 fps. Therefore

$$F_x = Q\rho\,\Delta V_x = \frac{5 \times 62.4 \times 150}{32.2}\ \text{lb}$$

and the power is

$$\frac{5 \times 62.4 \times 150 \times 200}{32.2 \times 550}\ \text{hp} = 528\ \text{hp}$$

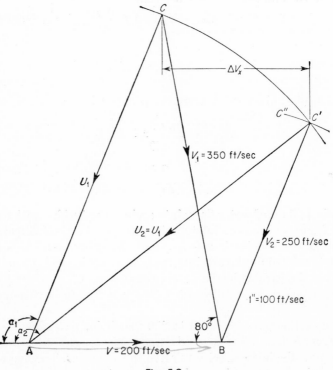

Fig. 5·9

Example 2: The blades of an impulse turbine have a peripheral velocity of 150 fps. Water flows into the turbine with an inlet velocity of 300 fps at 90° to the blade direction and out at an angle of 160° to the blade direction with a velocity of 175 fps. Calculate the turbine efficiency.

In this case U_1 and U_2 are not equal because friction is present; however, enough information is given to enable the velocity diagram (see Fig. 5·10) to be drawn directly.

From the diagram, $\Delta V_x = 165$ fps, and from Eq. (5·7),

$$\eta = \frac{2\,\Delta V_x\,v}{V_1{}^2 - V_2{}^2}$$

$$= \frac{2 \times 165 \times 150}{9 \times 10^4 - 3.05 \times 10^4}$$

$$= 0.831$$

Therefore the efficiency is 83.1 per cent.

Note: In this case, with V_1 at right angles to the blade direction, ΔV_x can be calculated directly as $V_2 \cos (180° - 160°)$.

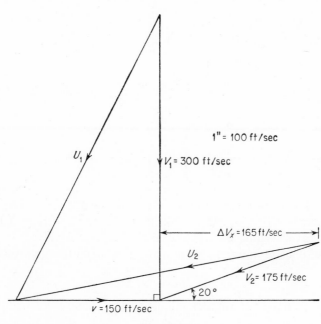

1" = 100 ft/sec

$V_1 = 300$ ft/sec

$\Delta V_x = 165$ ft/sec

$V_2 = 175$ ft/sec

$v = 150$ ft/sec

Fig. 5·10

5·5 Torque and the rate of change of angular momentum

Linear momentum was defined in Art. 5·1 as the product of the mass and the velocity of a moving body. *Angular momentum is similarly defined as the product of the moment of inertia and the angular velocity;* thus

$$\text{Angular momentum } M_A = I\omega \qquad\qquad (5\cdot8)$$

Inertia × w (angular velocity)

The rate of change of angular momentum is found by differentiating Eq. (5·8),

$$\frac{dM_A}{dt} = I \frac{d\omega}{dt} \tag{5·9}$$

The right-hand side of Eq. (5·9) is the familiar expression for torque T.

It is now possible to state the general angular-momentum equation thus: *The torque required to produce a change in angular velocity of a fluid is equal to the rate of change of angular momentum produced.*

Figure 5·11 shows a streamtube through which a flow of Q cfs is passing. Consider a small mass of fluid ΔM at station 1. This small mass reaches station 2 at a time Δt later. At station 1 the moment of inertia

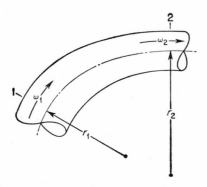

Fig. 5·11. A curved streamtube.

of the small mass about the center of rotation is $\Delta M \; r_1{}^2$, and its angular momentum is $\Delta M \; r_1{}^2\omega_1$. At station 2 the moment of inertia and momentum have become $\Delta M \; r_2{}^2$ and $\Delta M \; r_2{}^2\omega_2$ respectively.

The net change in angular momentum between these two stations is

$$\Delta M \; (r_1{}^2\omega_1 - r_2{}^2\omega_2)$$

The rate of change of angular momentum is then

$$\frac{\Delta M}{\Delta t} \; (r_1{}^2\omega_1 - r_2{}^2\omega_2)$$

but $\Delta M/\Delta t$ is the mass flowing per second and equals $Q\rho$. Therefore the applied torque is given by

$$T = Q\rho(r_1{}^2\omega_1 - r_2{}^2\omega_2) \tag{5·10}$$

Now $r_1\omega_1$ is equal to the tangential velocity component at station 1,

V_{t_1}, and $r_2\omega_2$ is equal to the tangential velocity component at station 2, V_{t_2}. So

$$T = Q\rho(r_1 V_{t_1} - r_2 V_{t_2}) \tag{5.11}$$

5·6   The reaction turbine

The reaction turbine, as opposed to the impulse turbine, is generally a more ponderous, slow-moving device, often developing very large power outputs. Hence it is used as the driving turbine in nearly all hydroelectric installations.

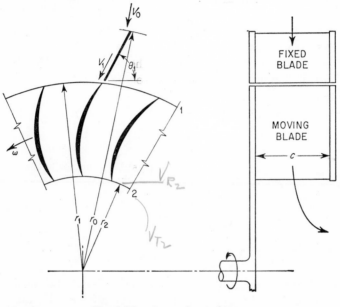

Fig. 5·12.   A reaction turbine.

It derives its power from the working fluid on an action and reaction basis, rather than by a simple momentum change, and causes a pressure drop in the working fluid, rather than a change of flow direction. The flow through a reaction turbine is a radial flow instead of the axial flow which occurs in an impulse turbine.

The essential parts of a reaction turbine are an outer fixed ring of stator blades and an inner moving ring of blades forming the rotor. The flow enters the stator all around its circumference and is discharged from the center of the rotor, as shown in Fig. 5·12.

The calculations involved in determining the performance of a reaction turbine may best be demonstrated by considering the typical turbine in Fig. 5·12.

The fluid entering the turbine is given an angular velocity, or swirl, by the stator blades and then enters the rotor. The fixed stator blades do no work since they are not in motion. The rotor reduces the angular velocity of the fluid (ideally, back to zero) and, in so doing, absorbs a torque from the fluid. This torque is available at the turbine output shaft.

The fluid enters the reaction turbine with a velocity V_0 which is considered to be entirely radial. This inlet velocity V_0 is related to the overall flow rate Q by the expression

$$Q = 2\pi r_0 c V_0$$

where r_0 = outer radius of stator

c = blade depth

After passing over the fixed blades, the fluid enters the rotor at an angle θ_1 to the blade direction with a velocity V_1 (greater than V_0 since

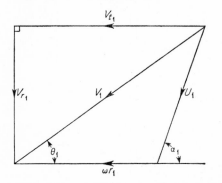

Fig. 5·13.   Reaction turbine inlet velocity diagram.

the radius is decreasing). This entry velocity V_1 may be considered the resultant of two vector components, V_{r_1} radially and V_{t_1} tangentially, as shown in Fig. 5·13. The radial velocity V_{r_1} is related to the flow rate by the expression

$$Q = 2\pi r_1 c V_{r_1} \qquad\qquad (5\cdot12a)$$

V_1 may also be considered the resultant of the blade velocity ωr_1 (ω = the angular velocity of the turbine) and the velocity of the fluid relative to the blade U_1, which is drawn to enter the blade smoothly at an angle α_1, the blade inlet angle. Compounding these, it is possible to draw a velocity diagram for blade entry conditions. A typical diagram is shown in Fig. 5·13.

Now at blade exit the radial velocity component V_{r_2} is given by

$$Q = 2\pi r_2 c V_{r_2} \qquad\qquad (5\cdot12b)$$

and the blade velocity by ωr_2.

The efflux velocity of the fluid relative to the blade U_2 must be drawn to leave the blade at an angle α_2, so that the angle α_2 is the blade exit angle shown in Fig. 5·14.

Now the resultant absolute velocity at exit V_2 may be considered the resultant of either the radial and tangential components V_{r_2} and V_{t_2} or the efflux velocity relative to the blade and the blade velocity, U_2 and ωr_2. The exit velocity diagram can now be drawn as shown in Fig. 5·14. In the case where the outlet swirl is zero, that is, $V_{t_2} = 0$, then $V_{r_2} = V_2$. The exit velocity diagram is as shown in Fig. 5·15.

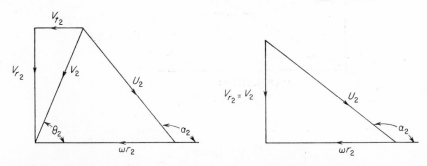

Fig. 5·14. Reaction turbine exit velocity diagram.

Fig. 5·15. Reaction turbine exit velocity diagram with zero swirl.

From these diagrams and Eq. (5·11), values may be found for V_{t_2} and V_{t_1}; hence the torque and power of the turbine may be calculated.

Example: 1,000 cfs of water is available to drive an industrial reaction turbine. The water enters the rotary stage at a radius of 6 ft at an angle of 30° to the blade direction. The blades are 1 ft deep.

Discharge takes place at a radius of 3.5 ft with no swirl. For a turbine speed of 50 rpm, calculate: (a) the required blade angles; (b) the horsepower output of the turbine; (c) the pressure drop across the turbine, neglecting the difference in exit and entry heights.

Calculating V_{r_1},

$$Q = 2\pi r_1 V_{r_1}$$

Therefore

$$V_{r_1} = \frac{Q}{2\pi r_1} = \frac{1,000}{12\pi} = 26.5 \text{ fps}$$

The blade velocity at entry is

$$\omega r_1 = \frac{50 \times 2\pi \times 6}{60} = 31.4 \text{ fps}$$

The absolute fluid entry angle is given as 30° to the blade direction, and so the entry velocity diagram can be drawn as shown in Fig. 5·16. From this diagram the blade entry angle is measured as 63°, the swirl velocity V_{t_1} as 45 fps, and the inlet velocity as 53 fps.

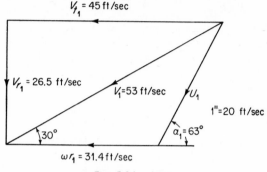

Fig. 5·16.   Inlet.

At outlet, $V_{t_2} = 0$. Therefore $V_2 = V_{r_2}$, which is found thus:

$$V_{r_2} = \frac{Q}{2\pi r_2} = \frac{1,000}{7\pi} = 45.4 \text{ fps}$$

At the outlet radius the blade velocity is given by

$$\omega r_2 = \frac{50 \times 2\pi \times 3.5}{60} = 18.3 \text{ fps}$$

Now the outlet velocity diagram can be drawn (see Fig. 5·17), and the

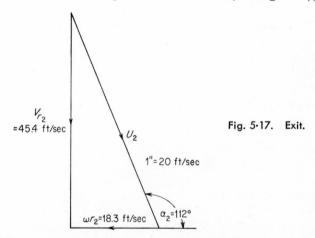

Fig. 5·17.   Exit.

blade outlet angle measured. This is found to be 112°.

The torque produced is given by

$$T = Q\rho(r_1 V_{t_1} - r_2 V_{t_2})$$
$$= \frac{1,000 \times 62.4 \times 6 \times 45}{32.2}$$
$$= 52,300 \text{ ft-lb}$$

Hence the horsepower developed is

$$\frac{52,300 \times 50 \times 2\pi}{33,000} = 4,980 \text{ hp}$$

Applying the energy equation across the turbine,

$$\frac{p_1}{\gamma} + \frac{V_1{}^2}{2g} + z_1 = \frac{p_2}{\gamma} + \frac{V_2{}^2}{2g} + z_2 + E_2$$

where E_2 is the energy extracted by the turbine per pound of fluid flowing and is given by

$$E_2 = \frac{\text{hp} \times 550}{Q\gamma}$$
$$= \frac{4,980 \times 550}{62,400} = 43.9 \text{ ft-lb/lb}$$

Now since $z_1 = z_2$,

$$\frac{p_1 - p_2}{\gamma} = \frac{V_2{}^2 - V_1{}^2}{2g} + E_2$$

Therefore
$$p_1 - p_2 = \gamma \left(E_2 - \frac{V_1{}^2 - V_2{}^2}{2g} \right)$$
$$= 62.4 \left(43.9 - \frac{53^2 - 45.4^2}{64.4} \right)$$
$$= 2,018 \text{ psf}$$
$$= 14.0 \text{ psi}$$

5·7   Jet propulsion

Jet propulsion is a simple application of the impulse-momentum equation and is effected by ejecting fluid momentum in the opposite direction to the required thrust. A very simple example is that of rocket thrust.

Consider a rocket which is using a total of M lb of fuel and oxidant per second and ejecting it at a velocity of V fps. In 1 sec an amount of burned fuel and oxidant is ejected with a momentum of MV/g lb-sec, and therefore the rate of change of momentum of the rocket is MV/g lb-sec/sec. The rate of change of momentum is equal to the thrust, and so

$$T = \frac{MV}{g} \quad \text{lb}$$

Example 1: A liquid-propellant rocket uses 22 lb of fuel per second and 300 lb of oxidant per second. The exhaust gases leave the rocket at 2,000 fps. Calculate the rocket thrust.

$$T = \frac{MV}{g}$$

$$= \frac{300 + 22}{32.2} \times 2,000 = 20,000 \text{ lb}$$

A more economical device for producing jet thrust is the air-breathing jet engine. Unlike the rocket, this does not need to carry its own

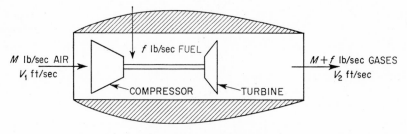

Fig. 5·18.   A jet engine.

oxidant, obtaining it from the air in which the engine operates. It is therefore strictly limited to use within the atmosphere. The principle of the jet engine is as follows:

1. Air is drawn into the front of the engine and compressed by a compressor.
2. Fuel is mixed with the air and the mixture ignited.
3. The resulting high-velocity gases are passed through an impulse turbine disk to extract the power required to drive the compressor.
4. The gases are exhausted to atmosphere with higher momentum than the intake air, thus creating thrust.

Consider the simple jet engine shown in Fig. 5·18. The engine is in motion at a speed of V_1 fps, but to clarify the calculations it is considered stationary in an airstream with a velocity of V_1 fps in the opposite direction. The exhaust gases leave the stationary engine with a final velocity of V_2 fps.

For an airflow rate of M lb/sec and a fuel flow rate of f lb/sec, the initial and final rates of momentum flow of the air and gases are

$$\text{Initial momentum rate} = \frac{MV_1}{g} \qquad \text{lb-sec/sec}$$

$$\text{Final momentum rate} = \frac{M+f}{g} V_2 \qquad \text{lb-sec/sec}$$

Therefore the rate of change of momentum is

$$\frac{M+f}{g} V_2 - \frac{MV_1}{g} \qquad \text{lb-sec/sec}$$

or thrust $$\qquad T = \frac{M+f}{g} V_2 - \frac{MV_1}{g} \qquad \text{lb} \qquad (5\cdot13)$$

Example 2: An aircraft traveling at 500 mph is propelled by a jet engine developing 8,000 lb thrust and operating with an air/fuel ratio of 25:1. If the exhaust velocity is 1,000 mph, find the required fuel flow rate.

Applying Eq. (5·13),

$$8,000 = \frac{(M+f) \times 1,000 \times 88}{g \times 60} - \frac{M \times 500 \times 88}{g \times 60}$$

But $M = 25f$; therefore

$$8,000 = \frac{26 \times f \times 1,000 \times 88}{60g} - \frac{25f \times 500 \times 88}{60g}$$

Hence $\qquad f = 12.95$ lb/sec

5·8 The ideal propeller disk

Complete airscrew theory is beyond the scope of this text, but some important general results may be obtained by considering the flow through a propeller disk (or actuator disk), which is a theoretical concept consisting simply of a disk that increases the momentum of the fluid passing through it without causing any rotation of the fluid. The results obtained by this method agree reasonably with those encountered practically.

Figure 5·19 shows an actuator disk moving through a fluid with a velocity V_1. This is essentially the same as a stationary disk in a flow of velocity V_1. The flow will accelerate as it approaches the disk, receive an energy increase in the form of a pressure rise in passing through the disk, and continue to accelerate downstream of the disk

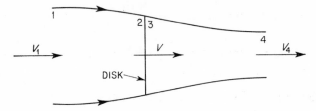

Fig. 5·19.   Flow through an ideal propeller disk.

until the pressure of the stream is the same as that of the free stream. The four stations indicated in Fig. 5·19 are

1. The free stream unaffected by the disk
2. Immediately ahead of the disk
3. Immediately behind the disk
4. Far downstream from the disk

Now $p_1 = p_4$, and since 2 and 3 are obviously very close together, $V_2 = V_3 = V$, say. The thrust developed is given by

$$T = (p_3 - p_2)A$$

where A is the disk area. Also, from Eq. (5·2)

$$T = Q\rho(V_4 - V_1)$$
$$= \rho A V(V_4 - V_1)$$

Therefore $$p_3 - p_2 = \rho V(V_4 - V_1) \qquad (5·14)$$

Applying Bernoulli's equation between stations 1 and 2 and between stations 3 and 4,

$$p_1 + \tfrac{1}{2}\rho V_1{}^2 = p_2 + \tfrac{1}{2}\rho V^2$$

and $$p_3 + \tfrac{1}{2}\rho V^2 = p_4 + \tfrac{1}{2}\rho V_4{}^2$$

Subtracting these two gives

$$p_3 - p_2 = p_4 + \tfrac{1}{2}\rho V_4{}^2 - p_1 - \tfrac{1}{2}\rho V_1{}^2$$
$$= \tfrac{1}{2}\rho(V_4{}^2 - V_1{}^2) \qquad (5·15)$$

Equating (5·14) and (5·15),

$$\tfrac{1}{2}\rho(V_4{}^2 - V_1{}^2) = \rho V(V_4 - V_1)$$

Therefore $$V = \frac{V_4 + V_1}{2} \qquad (5·16)$$

This indicates that the velocity through the disk is the mean of the initial and final velocities and that one-half of the acceleration takes place ahead of the propeller and the rest behind it.

5·9 Propeller efficiency

The power output P_o from the actuator disk is

$$P_o = TV_1 = Q\rho(V_4 - V_1)V_1$$

The power absorbed by the fluid P_i is given by

$$P_i = Q\gamma E$$

where E is the energy absorbed by the fluid per pound of fluid flowing. Since $p_1 = p_4$ and $z_1 = z_4$,

$$E = \frac{V_4{}^2 - V_1{}^2}{2g}$$

Hence
$$P_i = \frac{Q\gamma}{2g}(V_4{}^2 - V_1{}^2)$$
$$= \tfrac{1}{2}Q\rho(V_4 - V_1)(V_4 + V_1)$$
$$= \rho Q(V_4 - V_1)V$$

from Eq. (5·16). Therefore the propeller efficiency is

$$\eta = \frac{P_o}{P_i} = \frac{Q\rho(V_4 - V_1)V_1}{Q\rho(V_4 - V_1)V} = \boxed{\frac{V_1}{V}} \tag{5·17}$$

From Eq. (5·17) it will be seen that only an infinitely large propeller with $V_1 = V$ will operate at 100 per cent efficiency (or one developing no thrust!). Actual propellers usually have an efficiency of 80 to 90 per cent.

Example: Calculate the thrust and horsepower output of an aircraft propeller of 85 per cent efficiency and 7-ft diameter when traveling at 200 mph at sea level.

$$V_1 = 200 \text{ mph} = 293 \text{ fps}$$

Now
$$\frac{V_1}{V} = 0.85$$

therefore
$$V = \frac{293}{0.85} = 345 \text{ fps}$$

Hence
$$V_4 = 2V - V_1 = 397 \text{ fps}$$

The thrust is given by

$$T = \rho A V(V_4 - V_1) = \frac{0.00238 \times 49\pi \times 345 \times 104}{4} = 3,290 \text{ lb}$$

The horsepower output is

$$\frac{TV_1}{550} = \frac{3,290 \times 293}{550} = 1,755 \text{ hp}$$

PROBLEMS

5·1 A horizontal pipe contains a constriction which reduces the diameter from 4 to 2 in. Upstream of the constriction the pressure in the pipe is 17 psig, and 1.5 cfs of water is flowing in the pipe. Calculate the magnitude and direction of the force exerted on the constriction.

5·2 If the constriction of Prob. 5·1 is used as a nozzle in a system where the upstream pressure is maintained at 17 psig, estimate the magnitude and direction of the force exerted by the water on the nozzle.

5·3 The arm of a horizontally rotating lawn sprinkler contains water at a pressure of 6 psig. The end of the arm consists of a 90° bend and a nozzle reducing the diameter from 1 to ½ in. If 0.05 cfs of water passes through the nozzle, calculate the force exerted on it.

5·4 A vertical pipe 6 in. in diameter contains a conical expansion to 12-in. diameter; the expansion is 3 ft in length. The velocity of the water in the 6-in. pipe is 12 fps upward, and the pressure is 25 psig. Estimate the force exerted on the expansion.

5·5 The flow in a 3-in.-diameter pipe passes around a 100° horizontal bend. The velocity of the water in the pipe is 20 fps, and the pressure is 10 psig. Calculate the force exerted on the bend.

5·6 An impulse turbine with a blade velocity of 200 fps is driven by 0.1 slug of air per second entering with a velocity of 500 fps. If the inlet blade angle is 70° and the exit velocity is 250 fps, calculate the blade exit angle and the turbine output horsepower.

5·7 The turbine of Prob. 5·6 is to be coupled to a water supply so that the water leaves the turbine at right angles to the blade direction with a velocity of 100 fps. Find the new velocity for the turbine blades and the diameter of the inlet jet to give the same power output.

5·8 Fluid enters an impulse turbine at a rate of 0.08 slug/sec with a velocity of 400 fps at 45° to the blade direction. If the blade velocity is 200 fps and the flow is turned through an absolute angle of 90°, calculate the turbine efficiency when delivering 10 hp and the outlet velocity.

5·9 The exit fluid from the turbine of Prob. 5·8 flows directly into a coaxial contrarotating turbine with a peripheral velocity of 50 fps. Calculate the maximum recoverable horsepower in this turbine.

5·10 Two identical coaxial impulse turbines are separated by a row of stator blades and rotate with a common blade velocity of 250 fps. 2 cfs of water flows into the first turbine at 90° to the blade direction with a velocity of 350 fps. The blade outlet angle is 150°. Calculate the required stator blade angles and the horsepower output of the combination.

5·11 The flow of water into a reaction turbine is at a rate of 100 cfs at an angle of 25° to the blade direction. The blade angles are $\alpha_1 = 56°$ and $\alpha_2 = 100°$. The radius at entry to the rotor is 3 ft, and at discharge 1.5 ft. The blade depth is constant at 3 in. Find the running speed of the turbine, the torque, and the horsepower output.

103 RPM

5·12 A reaction turbine with inside and outside rotor diameters of 4 and 8 ft respectively and blades 6 in. deep is to develop 1,000 hp at 100 rpm from a supply of 150 cfs of water, exhausting the water with no swirl.   Calculate the required blade angles, the water inlet angle, and the minimum supply head required.

5·13 A centrifugal pump (basically a reaction turbine running in reverse) is to deliver 10 cfs of water at a radius of 1 ft. The water enters the rotor at a radius of 6 in., after leaving the preswirl stator at an angle of 45°, and leaves with no swirl. The blade height is 2 in. Calculate the horsepower required to drive the pump at 250 rpm and the pressure rise across the pump.

5·14 Assuming that the head of water is kept constant, calculate the jet thrust on the trolley shown in the figure.

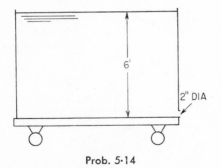

Prob. 5·14

5·15 A jet-propelled motorboat draws 15 cfs of water through ports in the boat's sides and discharges it astern through orifices with an effective area of 0.4 ft². If the boat travels at 10 mph, find the propulsive force.

5·16   A liquid fuel rocket uses 25 lb of fuel and 400 lb of oxidant per minute. The exhaust velocity is 1,000 fps. Calculate the thrust delivered.

If the rocket has a structural weight of 50 lb and a fuel and oxidant load of 106.5 lb, find the terminal velocity of the rocket when fired vertically. (Neglect air resistance.)

5·17   An aircraft turbojet engine swallows 40,000 cfs of air at an altitude where the density of the air is 0.0006 slug/ft^3 at a speed of 400 mph. Calculate the exhaust velocity required to produce a thrust of 8,000 lb with an air/fuel ratio of 17:1.

5·18   An 8-ft-diameter propeller operating at sea level at 200 mph produces a thrust of 2,000 lb. Calculate its efficiency and the engine power required.

5·19   Calculate the thrust and engine power required to drive a ship at 15 mph with a propeller of 3-ft diameter and 80 per cent efficiency.

CHAPTER 6

Dimensional Analysis and
Model Similarity

The process of checking the dimensions of every term of an equation for consistency is probably a familiar one; for instance, the addition of an area to a volume is meaningless since area and volume are dimensionally incompatible. Areas may only be added to or equated with other areas and volumes with volumes. In other words, each side of an equation must have both the same numerical value *and* the same dimensions if the equation is to be consistent. This leads to the subject of dimensional analysis—a very powerful, empirical tool in the study of fluid mechanics and many other subjects.

6·1 Systems of dimensions

The two most common systems of dimensions currently in use are the force-length-time-temperature and the mass-length-time-temperature systems, referred to as the $FLT\theta$ and $MLT\theta$ systems. Since the distinction between pounds of force and pounds of mass seems to be confusing, *the $MLT\theta$ system of dimensions will be used here.* In this system the dimensions of force are obtained from Newton's second law, $F = Ma$, which is to say that force has units of mass times acceleration.

Table 6·1 shows the $MLT\theta$ dimensions of some of the parameters common in the field of fluid mechanics.

6·2 The method of dimensional analysis

Consider the case of a fluid discharge from a hole in the side of a large tank of fluid. The velocity of the discharge is given by

$$V = \sqrt{2gh} \qquad\qquad (3.7)$$

Examining the dimensions of this equation for equality,

$$LT^{-1} = (LT^{-2}L)^{1/2} = LT^{-1}$$

shows that the equation is dimensionally consistent.

Suppose now that Eq. (3·7) was not known. The method of dimensional analysis makes it possible to deduce the equation empirically, provided that the dependent variables can be correctly assumed.

Table 6·1 $MLT\theta$ dimensions of some common variables

Quantity	Symbol	Dimensions
Length	L	L
Time	t	T
Mass	M	M
Temperature	θ	θ
Force	F	MLT^{-2}
Velocity	v	LT^{-1}
Acceleration	a	LT^{-2}
Area	A	L^2
Volume	V	L^3
Flow rate	Q	L^3T^{-1}
Weight flow rate	G	MLT^{-3}
Mass flow rate	G	MT^{-1}
Pressure	p	$ML^{-1}T^{-2}$
Density	ρ	ML^{-3}
Specific weight	γ	$ML^{-2}T^{-2}$
Specific gravity	S	None
Dynamic viscosity	μ	$ML^{-1}T^{-1}$
Kinematic viscosity	ν	L^2T^{-1}
Bulk modulus	K	$ML^{-1}T^{-2}$
Gas constant	R	$L\theta^{-1}$

Deciding upon the correct variables is the most difficult part of the analysis, but with careful reasoning and a little experience, incorrect assumptions will be eliminated.

In this case it can be seen that the velocity may depend solely upon:

1. The height h of the fluid head above the hole

2. The type of fluid, represented by its density ρ

3. The acceleration due to gravity, g

Since the fluid is considered ideal, all the viscosity terms may be neglected.

Thus the equation for the velocity from such an orifice may be written as

$$V = \text{const } h^a \rho^b g^c$$

where the indices a, b, and c are constants to be determined by considering the dimensional balance of the equation.

The dimensions of the left-hand term are LT^{-1} and of the right-hand terms are $L^a(ML^{-3})^b(LT^{-2})^c$. Equating these gives

$$LT^{-1} = L^a(ML^{-3})^b(LT^{-2})^c$$

For the length dimensions to balance,

$$1 = a - 3b - 2c$$

and for the mass dimensions,

$$0 = b$$

and for the time dimensions,

$$-1 = -2c$$

Solving these three simultaneous equations gives

$$a = \tfrac{1}{2} \qquad b = 0 \qquad c = \tfrac{1}{2}$$

and so
$$V = \text{const } \sqrt{gh}$$

Note that although fluid density was assumed to be one of the variables in this case, the analysis eliminated it, showing that the discharge rate is independent of fluid density. This will not always happen and, generally, too many variables will complicate the analysis. If four or more variables are involved, unnecessary ones will not be eliminated; thus *it is extremely important to include every relevant variable, but to avoid unnecessary ones at all costs.* This is a technique which can only be learned with practice and experience.

There are two definite limitations to the method of dimensional analysis. Firstly, it will not determine the value of the constant which occurs in all expressions derived by this method; and secondly, it will only analyze the problem completely if four or less variables are involved. (Three, if the temperature is not included.)

The advantage of the method is not, then, in complete mathematical analysis, but rather in application to experiment, since the method indicates the type of variation to be expected.

For the case outlined above, dimensional analysis indicates that a plot of velocity against the square root of the head should be a straight line, and from this plot the value of the constant can be determined.

6·3 The elimination of variables in a system of four or more variables

If a system is examined in which four or more variables are present, the method of dimensional analysis makes it possible to reduce the number of variables by grouping terms together as dimensionless quantities. For example, the force exerted on a body moving through an incompressible fluid may be established as follows.

The value of the force depends solely upon:

1. The size of the object, represented by a typical length, L
2. The relative velocity between the fluid and the object, v
3. The fluid density, ρ
4. The fluid viscosity, ν
5. The acceleration due to gravity, g

Thus the equation can be written as

$$F = \text{const } L^a v^b \rho^c \nu^d g^e \qquad (6\cdot1)$$

and dimensionally

$$MLT^{-2} = L^a(LT^{-1})^b(ML^{-3})^c(L^2T^{-1})^d(LT^{-2})^e$$

Examining each of the dimensions individually,

M: $1 = c$

L: $1 = a + b + 2d - 3c + e$

T: $-2 = -b - d - 2e$

Solving these in terms of d and e,

$$c = 1$$
$$b = 2 - d - 2e$$
$$a = 4 - 2d - e - b = 2 - d + e$$

so that Eq. (6·1) can be written as

$$F = \text{const } L^{2-d+e}\, v^{2-d-2e} \rho^c \nu^d g^e \qquad (6\cdot2)$$

and therefore
$$F = \text{const }\left(\frac{vL}{\nu}\right)^{-d}\left(\frac{v^2}{gL}\right)^{-e} \rho v^2 L^2 \qquad (6\cdot3)$$

where the terms in parenthesis are dimensionless.

6·4   Reynolds number and Froude number

In Eq. (6·3) there were two dimensionless quantities, vL/ν and v^2/gL. The first of these is called the *Reynolds number* after the British physicist O. Reynolds and is a number of extreme importance in fluid mechanics. It is particularly important in the evaluation of model test results and their extrapolation to full-scale prediction. The second quantity is called the *Froude number* and has particular significance in the evaluation of test results involving surface movements and wave drag.

If two geometrically similar models of different scale are entirely immersed in and moving through two different fluids, then the flow patterns existing around each model are geometrically similar if the Reynolds numbers of the two flows are the same.

If the motions take place in the surface of the two fluids and wave motions are involved, then the wave patterns will be similar if the Froude numbers of the two flows are equal.

$$\text{Reynolds number } N_R = \frac{vL}{\nu} \qquad (6\cdot4)$$

$$\text{Froude number } N_F = \frac{v^2}{gL} \qquad (6\cdot5)$$

Hence Eq. (6·3) can be written as

$$F = f(N_R, N_F)\rho v^2 L^2 \qquad (6\cdot6)$$

or more usually

$$F = C_F \tfrac{1}{2}\rho v^2 L^2 \qquad \mathbf{(6\cdot7)}$$

where C_F is the force coefficient and is given by

$$C_F = 2f(N_R, N_F) \qquad (6\cdot8)$$

6·5   The use of models and the extrapolation of the results to full-scale prediction

From Eq. (6·7) it will be seen that in order to predict forces arising from fluid movement over a solid body, the force coefficient C_F must be known. This could be found by measuring the force on the object under known and controlled conditions, such as those existing in a wind tunnel, but the disadvantages of this are apparent when applied to something as large as an aircraft. In such a case it is obviously advantageous to measure the forces on an inexpensive model and use the results to determine the final forces on the full-scale aircraft, thus possibly avoiding expensive errors.

The problem is simplified by the use of models, usually smaller than full-scale, but not necessarily so. Unfortunately, however, mere geometrical similarity is not sufficient. As Eq. (6·6) shows, the Reynolds number and the Froude number for the model must be the same as for the full-scale object if the results are to be exactly coordinated. In practice this is seldom achieved since similarity is maintained between Froude numbers for problems in which surface effects (such as waves) occur and between Reynolds numbers otherwise.

Many ingenious methods have been devised to achieve similarity between model and full-scale effects. The most common of these are the compressed air wind tunnel and the water tunnel. Both are used so that variation between model and full-scale velocities can be compensated for by a variation in fluid density and viscosity.

Example 1: A one-fifth scale model of an airplane is tested in (a) a wind tunnel, and (b) a water tunnel. Calculate the tunnel speeds required to correspond to a full-scale speed of 100 fps at sea level.

$$N_{R_{\text{model}}} = N_{R_{\text{full scale}}}$$

Therefore
$$\frac{v_m L_m}{\nu_m} = \frac{v_f L_f}{\nu_f}$$

or
$$v_m = v_f \frac{\nu_m}{\nu_f} \frac{L_f}{L_m}$$

$$= 5 \frac{\nu_m}{\nu_f} v_f = 500 \frac{\mu_m}{\mu_f} \frac{\rho_f}{\rho_m}$$

(a) In the wind tunnel, $\mu_m = \mu_f$ and $\rho_m = \rho_f$, and so

$$v_m = 500 \text{ fps}$$

(b) In the water tunnel,

$$\mu_m = 2.1 \times 10^{-5} \text{ lb-sec/ft}^2$$
$$\mu_f = 0.0377 \times 10^{-5} \text{ lb-sec/ft}^2$$
$$\rho_f = 0.00238 \text{ slug/ft}^3$$
$$\rho_m = 1.94 \text{ slugs/ft}^3$$

Therefore
$$v_m = 500 \frac{2.1}{0.0377} \frac{0.00238}{1.94}$$

$$= 34.2 \text{ fps}$$

Example 2: A 5-ft model of a ship 200 ft long is tested in a tank of fluid with a specific gravity of 0.9 and a viscosity of 4.2×10^{-6} lb-sec/ft². Calculate the model velocity to give the same wave pattern as the full-scale pattern at 30 fps and the ratio of the Reynolds numbers at this speed.

For identical wave patterns the Froude numbers must be the same:

$$\frac{v_m^2}{L_m g} = \frac{v_f^2}{L_f g}$$

Therefore
$$v_m = v_f \sqrt{\frac{L_m}{L_f}} = 4.75 \text{ fps}$$

The ratio of the Reynolds numbers is

$$\frac{N_{R_f}}{N_{R_m}} = \frac{v_f L_f v_m}{v_m L_m v_f}$$

$$= \frac{30 \times 200}{4.75 \times 5} \frac{\mu_m}{\mu_f} \frac{\rho_f}{\rho_m}$$

$$= 253 \times \frac{4.2 \times 10^{-6}}{2.1 \times 10^{-5}} \times \frac{1}{0.9}$$

$$= 56.3$$

PROBLEMS

6·1 Use the method of dimensional analysis to derive the relationship for pressure intensity at a depth h in a fluid of density ρ.

6·2 Use the method of dimensional analysis to derive the relationship for the excess pressure within a soap bubble.

6·3 Use the method of dimensional analysis to derive the relationship for the shear stress in the fluid between two closely spaced, relatively moving plates.

6·4 Use the method of dimensional analysis to show that mach number can be expressed as

$$M = f\left(\frac{\rho V^2}{K}\right)$$

where K is the bulk modulus.

6·5 Use the method of dimensional analysis to show that the force on a body moving in a compressible fluid can be expressed as

$$F = F(M, N_R, N_F)\rho v^2 L^2$$

6·6 A test representing flight at an altitude of 20,000 ft is to be carried out in a compressed air wind tunnel on a one-tenth scale model of an airplane. What should the tunnel pressure be in atmospheres?

6·7 The lift force on an airfoil of one-sixteenth full scale in an atmospheric wind tunnel with a speed of 100 fps was found to be 4.00 lb. Calculate the lift force on the full-scale airfoil, with similar geometry at 200 fps at 40,000 ft, neglecting any variation in Reynolds number.

6·8 A one-twentieth scale model seaplane hull is tested in a freshwater tank at a speed of 12.5 fps. What speed does this represent for the full-scale hull in seawater? What is the ratio of the full-scale Reynolds number to that of the model?

6·9   A model of a water main, running full, is to be made to one-twentieth scale, using gasoline as the fluid. Calculate the velocity ratio required for dynamic similarity.

6·10   A one-sixteenth scale model of an automobile is tested in a water tunnel. Calculate the water velocity to give dynamic similarity between the model and the full-scale vehicle moving at 60 mph.

If the force exerted on the model in the tunnel is 1,000 lb, calculate the horsepower required by the vehicle to overcome air resistance at 60 mph.

6·11   An object which moves wholly in air is model-tested in a water tunnel. What model scale must be used to give *complete* dynamic similarity (i.e., correct Reynolds *and* Froude numbers)? What will be the model velocity?

6·12   A ship designed to travel at 30 mph is 450 ft long. At what speed should a 10-ft-long model be towed through water to give dynamic similarity?

If the force required to tow the model at this speed is 1.10 lb, calculate the horsepower required by the ship when traveling at 30 mph.

CHAPTER 7

Viscous Resistance to Fluid Flow

In most of the previous analysis, ideal fluids were assumed, and the effects due to friction were ignored. In this chapter the effects of viscous resistance will be discussed. This does not render all the earlier analysis obsolete; it simply points out the fact that the results will not be entirely accurate unless friction is considered. In most of the previous work the conduits were short and the fluids not very viscous, with the result that the frictional effects were indeed small and justifiably negligible. However, if the fluids are of high viscosity or if the conduits are of considerable length, as assumed in this chapter, then the frictional effects cannot be ignored.

7·1 The nature of laminar and turbulent flows

If a fluid flows in such a manner that any two small particles of fluid, close together, move along two smooth nonintersecting streamlines, the flow is said to be *laminar*. In such a flow the fluid may be considered to be moving in a series of layers or laminae of molecular thickness, each layer sliding smoothly over the layer adjacent to it.

If the velocity of a flow reaches a high enough value, the flow ceases to be laminar and becomes *turbulent*. In this type of flow, the velocity at a point in the flow is seen to be a random, continually changing vector, the time average of which is the mean velocity of the flow. The random variations consist of small-amplitude high-frequency perturbations both along and across the flow direction, superimposed upon a steady mean velocity in the flow direction. These are shown in Fig. 7·1. The velocity V_x is measured in the direction of flow and can be seen to average to the mean velocity V; the velocity across the flow direction V_y can be seen to average zero.

In laminar flow, a fluid particle at a point in the flow is constrained to move in the lamina containing that point. However, in turbulent flow there are no "layers," the fluid becoming thoroughly mixed in

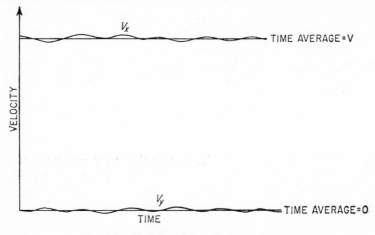

Fig. 7·1.   Turbulent flow velocity variations.

flowing and the turbulent eddies causing a considerable increase in resistance to flow.

7·2 The critical Reynolds number

In 1883 Reynolds performed the now classic experiment to determine the conditions governing the transition from laminar to turbulent flow. Using the apparatus shown in Fig. 7·2, he allowed the fluid from the large tank to flow through a bell-mouthed entrance and along a smooth glass tube, controlling the flow by means of a valve at the end. A capillary tube connected to a reservoir of dye allowed the introduction of a filament of dye into the flow stream.

While the flow in the tube remained laminar, the dye filament remained steady. But when turbulence occurred, the dye filament became ragged and dispersed, eventually completely mixing with the main fluid.

Reynolds found that with care, laminar flow could be maintained until the flow Reynolds number reached 12,000, a value which has since been extended to 40,000—50,000 by allowing the fluid in the tank to stand for several days prior to the experiment and by making sure that the apparatus is entirely free from vibration. This value is called the *upper critical Reynolds number*. It has little or no significance in engineering since flows do not generally take place under such well-controlled conditions. As far as the engineer is concerned, all flows with a Reynolds number higher than 4,000 are likely to be turbulent.

Once turbulence has started, laminar flow may only be reestablished by reducing the flow Reynolds number to the *lower critical Reynolds*

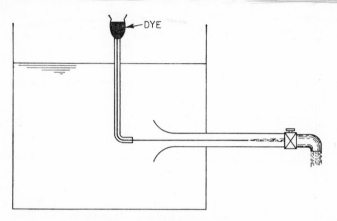

Fig. 7·2. Reynolds' experiment.

number, a value of approximately 2,000. This value does have a practical application in that *all flows with a Reynolds number less than 2,000 will always be laminar*.

Thus all flows may be grouped into three regions by Reynolds number:

1. Less than 2,000: Laminar flow region
2. Between 2,000 and 4,000: Transition region in which the flow may be laminar or turbulent, but in which a disturbance will cause transition from laminar to turbulent flow
3. Greater than 4,000: Turbulent flow region

7·3 The boundary layer

In Art. 1·4 it was pointed out that in the flow of real fluids the velocity of the fluid close to a solid boundary is exactly equal to the velocity of the boundary, so that no relative motion exists between the boundary and the layer of fluid next to it. This causes the fluid to have a velocity profile close to a boundary as shown in Fig. 1·5, the velocity of the fluid increasing with distance from the boundary, causing shearing stresses to be present within the fluid.

The velocity gradient and the resulting shearing stresses cause friction losses to occur within the region of a flow close to a boundary; this important region of varying velocity is termed the *boundary layer*. The study of the boundary layer is a subject in itself, and no attempt will be made here to analyze the flow within the boundary layer, other than in an elementary fashion.

The boundary layer is not a separate part of a flow in that it has no actual physical limit, but it is generally defined as the region in which the flow velocity is less than 99 per cent of the maximum velocity of that flow, as shown in Fig. 7·3. In other words, it is the region in which

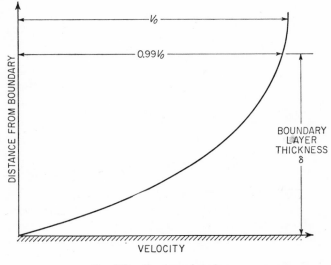

Fig. 7·3. The boundary layer.

all but a very small fraction of the viscous losses occur. Outside the boundary layer, the velocity variation and the resulting shear stresses are negligible.

The thickness of the boundary layer varies considerably from application to application. On the surface of a high-speed aircraft wing the thickness of the boundary layer is of the order of hundredths of an inch, whereas in a fully established flow in a pipe the boundary layer fills the pipe completely.

Although the boundary layer is *not* a separate part of the flow, it does act like a thin, pliable film placed on the surface of a solid boundary. Free stream pressures are transmitted unchanged across this film, but adverse pressure gradients, that is, pressures which increase in the downstream direction—usually associated with decelerating flow, can cause the boundary layer to separate from the solid boundary, causing a wake to form with considerable increase in drag. Such a flow condition occurs when a real fluid flows round a circular cylinder.

Figure 7·4a shows the flow of an ideal fluid around a two-dimensional circular cylinder, in which the flow pattern is symmetrical about the center of the cylinder. Figure 7·4b shows the flow of a real fluid around the same cylinder. In passing around the cylinder, the flow accelerates until the maximum displacement position is reached, causing the pressure to drop up to this point. After this position is reached, the flow decelerates to reach the free stream velocity far downstream, resulting in an adverse pressure gradient over the rear of the cylinder which eventually causes the boundary layer to break away from the cylinder

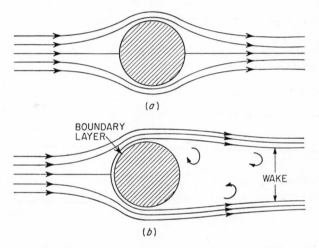

Fig. 7·4. Flow round a two-dimensional cylinder.

to form a wake. Since the boundary layer is a region of a real flow (in which the velocity is less than 99 per cent of the maximum flow velocity), it too may be laminar or turbulent, according to the flow Reynolds number.

The laminar boundary layer, by its nature, offers less resistance to flow than the turbulent layer, but is less stable. In the presence of an adverse pressure gradient, a laminar boundary layer will always separate from a boundary before a turbulent one, and for this reason artificial means are often used to cause the transition from a laminar to a turbulent boundary layer before the onset of an adverse pressure gradient.

Figure 7·5 shows how two strips of thin wire placed along a two-dimensional circular cylinder cause the boundary layer to become

turbulent just before the onset of the adverse pressure gradient. The
turbulent boundary layer will adhere to the surface longer than the

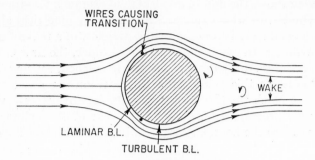

Fig. 7·5.   Artificially produced transition.

laminar boundary layer, resulting in a rather narrower wake, with a
net drag less than for the all-laminar flow case.

7·4   Laminar flow analyzed

The basic equation of laminar flow,

$$\tau = \mu \frac{dv}{dy} \tag{1·3}$$

was established in Art. 1·4 by considering the laminar flow of a fluid
past a solid boundary, and no consideration was given at that time to
the possibility of the flow being turbulent. It must now be emphasized

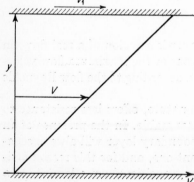

**Fig. 7·6.   Velocity distribution between
parallel flat plates in relative motion.**

that the equation is true only if the flow is laminar, that is to say, if
the flow Reynolds number is less than 2,000. Provided that this condition is observed, Eq. (1·3) may be used to analyze the various types of
laminar flow that occur.

$$N_R = \frac{Vd}{F} = \frac{Vd\gamma}{\mu g}$$

Laminar flow between relatively moving, parallel flat plates. This case may best be considered by assuming one plate to be stationary and the other to be moving with a velocity V_1 as shown in Fig. 7·6. The shear stress at each plate is equal and opposite, and so the shear must be transmitted unchanged across the gap. It can be seen, then, that the value of τ, and hence dv/dy, is constant across the gap, resulting in the linear velocity variation shown in Fig. 7·6.

Example: A flat plate 3 ft² in area moves edgewise through oil between two large fixed parallel planes, 1 in. from one and 3 in. from the other, as shown in Fig. 7·7. If the velocity of the plate is 2 fps and the oil has

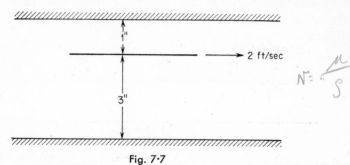

$$N = \frac{\mu}{\varsigma}$$

Fig. 7·7

a kinematic viscosity of 5×10^{-4} ft²/sec and a specific gravity of 0.8, calculate the drag force on the plate.

Establishing the Reynolds number for the flow between the plate and the most remote wall,

$$N_R = \frac{Vd}{\nu} = \frac{2 \times 3}{12 \times 5 \times 10^{-4}} = 1{,}000$$

and since the Reynolds number of the second flow is less than this, both the flows are laminar.

There will be a drag force on both sides of the plate, and solving for these separately,

$$\tau_1 = \mu \frac{V}{\frac{1}{12}}$$

$$= 12V\rho\nu$$

$$= \frac{12 \times 2 \times 0.8 \times 62.4 \times 5 \times 10^{-4}}{32.2}$$

$$= 0.0186 \text{ psf}$$

and

$$\tau_2 = \mu \frac{V}{\frac{3}{12}}$$

$$= 0.0062 \text{ psf}$$

Hence the net force on the plate is

$$3(0.0186 + 0.0062) = 0.0744 \text{ lb}$$

Laminar flow between flat, parallel stationary boundaries. For this type of flow the velocity distribution must be of the form indicated in Fig. 7·8, which is to say that the velocity must be zero at both plates and a maximum at the center. In order to maintain flow against the resulting viscous resistance, a force in the form of a pressure differential or a potential drop must exist.

Consider the equilibrium of the element shown in Fig. 7·8. The element is centered on the flow center line for symmetry and is of unit depth, so that the viscous force on the element is $2\tau\,dx$. The net

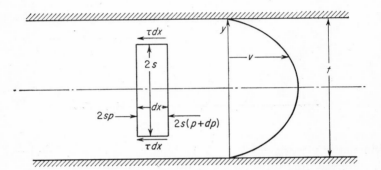

Fig. 7·8.   Velocity distribution between parallel stationary flat plates.

pressure force on the element is $2s\,dp$ in the same direction, and for equilibrium

$$2s\,dp + 2\tau\,dx = 0$$

Therefore $\tau = -s\dfrac{dp}{dx} = \mu\dfrac{dv}{dy}$ for laminar flow

Now at any section the pressure is constant *across* the flow; hence

$$v = -\frac{1}{\mu}\frac{dp}{dx}\int s\,dy = \frac{1}{\mu}\frac{dp}{dx}\int s\,ds \qquad \text{since } s = \frac{t}{2} - y$$

Therefore $v = \dfrac{1}{\mu}\dfrac{dp}{dx}\left(\dfrac{s^2}{2} + c\right)$

But when $s = \pm t/2$, $v = 0$. So $c = -t^2/8$ and

$$v = \frac{1}{\mu}\frac{dp}{dx}\left(\frac{s^2}{2} - \frac{t^2}{8}\right) \tag{7·1}$$

which is the equation to a parabola. Thus the velocity distribution across the flow is parabolic, and the maximum velocity is at the center where $s = 0$. So

$$v_{max} = -\frac{1}{\mu}\frac{dp}{dx}\frac{t^2}{8}$$ (7·2)

The maximum velocity is of only academic interest, the mean or average velocity having more significance. So, since the area of a parabola is two-thirds of the area of the surrounding rectangle,

$$V = \tfrac{2}{3}v_{max} = -\frac{t^2}{12\mu}\frac{dp}{dx}$$ (7·3)

which can be rearranged to establish the pressure drop; thus

$$\int_2^1 dp = -\int_2^1 \frac{12\mu V}{t^2}\,dx$$

Therefore

$$p_1 - p_2 = -\frac{12\mu V}{t^2}(x_1 - x_2)$$

$$= +\frac{12\mu V}{t^2}(x_2 - x_1)$$

$$= \frac{12\mu VL}{t^2}$$ (7·4)

which represents the pressure drop due to laminar friction. Including this term in the incompressible form of Bernoulli's equation gives

$$\frac{p_1}{\gamma} + z_1 + \frac{V_1^2}{2g} - \left(\frac{p_2}{\gamma} + z_2 + \frac{V_2^2}{2g}\right) = \frac{12\mu VL}{\gamma t^2}$$ (7·5)

Example: 0.05 cfs of water ($\nu = 1.25 \times 10^{-5}$ ft²/sec) flows between two smooth parallel plates 0.3 in. apart and 3 ft in width. Calculate the maximum velocity and the pressure 180 ft upstream from an atmospheric discharge if the upstream point is 3 ft higher than the discharge (see Fig. 7·9).

$$\text{Flow area} = \frac{3 \times 0.3}{12} = 0.075 \text{ ft}^2$$

Therefore

$$V = \frac{Q}{A} = \frac{0.05}{0.075} = 0.67 \text{ fps}$$

Hence the Reynolds number is

$$\frac{0.67 \times 0.3}{12 \times 1.25 \times 10^{-5}} = 1,330$$

below 2,000

and so the flow is laminar.

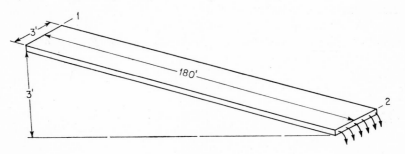

Fig. 7·9

Now from Eq. (7·3)

$$v_{max} = \tfrac{3}{2}V = 1.0 \text{ fps}$$

and from Eq. (7·5)

atmospheric

$P_2 = 14.7$

$$\frac{p_1}{\gamma} + 3 = \frac{12\mu VL}{\gamma t^2} = \frac{12\nu VL}{gt^2}$$

$$= \frac{12 \times 1.25 \times 10^{-5} \times 0.67 \times 180}{\left(\dfrac{0.3}{12}\right)^2 \times 32.2}$$

$$= 0.895$$

and so

$$\frac{p_1}{\gamma} = 0.895 - 3 = -2.105 \text{ ft}$$

pressure drop

or

$$p_1 = \frac{2.105 \times 12}{13.55} \text{ in. mercury vacuum}$$

sign vacuum

$$= 1.78 \text{ in. mercury vacuum}$$

Laminar flow through circular pipes. Consideration of this flow shows that around the circumference of the pipe the velocity is zero and that the maximum velocity occurs along the center line of the flow. The equation of the velocity profile may be obtained by considering the forces acting on a cylindrical element of radius r placed symmetrically about the pipe center line, as shown in Fig. 7·10. The viscous force acting on the element is $\tau 2\pi r\, dx$, and the net pressure force is $dp\,\pi r^2$

acting in the same direction. Hence, for equilibrium,

$$2\pi r \tau \, dx + dp \, \pi r^2 = 0$$

Therefore $\qquad \tau = -\dfrac{dp}{dx}\dfrac{r}{2} = \mu\dfrac{dv}{dy} \qquad$ for laminar flow

Now at any cross section the pressure is constant *across* the flow; hence

$$v = -\frac{1}{2\mu}\frac{dp}{dx}\int r \, dy = +\frac{1}{2\mu}\frac{dp}{dx}\int r \, dr \qquad \text{since } r = D/2 - y$$

Therefore $\qquad\qquad v = \dfrac{1}{2\mu}\dfrac{dp}{dx}\left(\dfrac{r^2}{2} + c\right)$

But $v = 0$ when $r = D/2$. Therefore $c = -D^2/8$ and

$$v = \frac{1}{2\mu}\frac{dp}{dx}\left(\frac{r^2}{2} - \frac{D^2}{8}\right) \tag{7.6}$$

The maximum velocity occurs when $r = 0$, and so

$$v_{\max} = -\frac{D^2}{16\mu}\frac{dp}{dx} \tag{7.7}$$

Again the maximum value is of little practical value, the mean velocity having more physical significance. Since the volume of a paraboloid

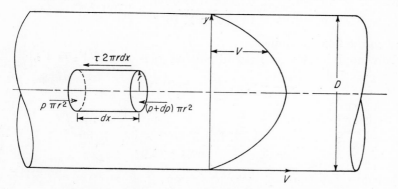

Fig. 7·10. Velocity distribution across a circular pipe.

is one-half the volume of the surrounding cylinder, it is apparent that

$$V = \frac{1 v_{\max}}{2} = -\frac{D^2}{32\mu}\frac{dp}{dx} \tag{7.8}$$

Now solving for the pressure drop,

$$\int_2^1 dp = -\int_2^1 \frac{32\mu V}{D^2}\, dx$$

Therefore
$$p_1 - p_2 = -\frac{32\mu V}{D^2}(x_1 - x_2)$$

$$= \frac{32\mu V}{D^2}(x_2 - x_1)$$

$$= \frac{32\mu VL}{D^2} \qquad (7\cdot9)$$

and since this is the pressure drop due to laminar friction, Bernoulli's equation can be written as

$$\frac{p_1}{\gamma} + \frac{V_1^2}{2g} + z_1 - \frac{p_2}{\gamma} - \frac{V_2^2}{2g} - z_2 = \frac{32\mu VL}{\gamma D^2} \qquad (7\cdot10)$$

Example: If 0.15 cfs of oil of viscosity 120×10^{-5} lb-sec/ft^2 and specific gravity 0.92 flows through a straight 2-in.-diameter smooth pipe, calculate the pipe gradient to give constant pressure along the pipe.

$$V = \frac{Q}{A} = \frac{144 \times 0.15}{\pi} = 6.87 \text{ fps}$$

Hence the Reynolds number is

$$\frac{0.92 \times 62.4 \times 6.87 \times 2}{32.2 \times 120 \times 12 \times 10^{-5}} = 1{,}700$$

and so the flow is laminar.

Now applying Eq. (7·10) and putting $p_1 = p_2$ and $V_1 = V_2$,

$$z_1 - z_2 = \frac{32\mu VL}{\gamma D^2}$$

so that for $L = 1$ ft,

$$z_1 - z_2 = \frac{32 \times 120 \times 10^{-5} \times 6.87 \times 36}{62.4 \times 0.92}$$

$$= 0.166 \text{ ft}$$

which is to say that the gradient of the pipe must be 0.166.

7·5　The velocity distribution in turbulent flow

A large majority of the flows encountered in engineering are flows at high Reynolds numbers, and so are turbulent. Unfortunately, the complex nature of turbulent flow does not allow complete mathematical analysis of the flow, which is possible for laminar flows. Most of the equations used in turbulent analysis are obtained from experimental data, vast quantities of which are available.

Close to a solid boundary in a turbulent flow, the combined effect of reduced velocity and the restraining influence of the boundary results in a thin region of laminar flow close to the boundary. This layer, always present, is called the laminar sublayer. The transition from laminar to turbulent flow across this region is not sudden so that, although the laminar sublayer is thin, it does not have a definite limit.

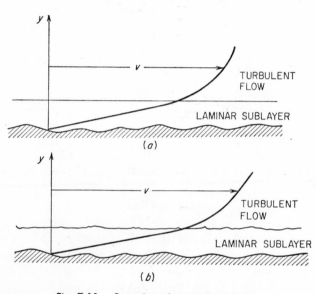

Fig. 7·11.   Smooth and rough boundaries.

The velocity distribution across the laminar sublayer is parabolic, but is so thin that a linear velocity profile may be assumed to exist across it without undue error.

In laminar flow all surfaces may be assumed smooth as the surface finish does not affect the fluid resistance. A boundary may be considered smooth in turbulent flow only if the effects of surface roughness do not extend beyond the laminar sublayer. Thus a surface may be either smooth or rough, depending on the width of the laminar sublayer, which in turn depends on the flow Reynolds number.

Figure 7·11a shows turbulent flow over a smooth surface. The effects of surface roughness do not extend beyond the edge of the laminar sublayer, which is seen to have a smooth edge. In Fig. 7·11b the surface roughness is such that the effects of it are transmitted through the laminar sublayer and extended into the region of fully developed turbulent flow, so that this surface must be considered rough.

The actual shape of the velocity profile in turbulent flow is hard to analyze, but experiment shows it to be flatter than the laminar one, with a laminar profile close to the wall (see Fig. 7·12). Experimental results show that the average velocity and the maximum velocity in

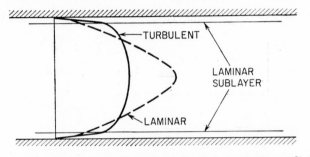

Fig. 7·12.   Comparison of laminar and turbulent velocity profiles.

fully developed turbulent flow within a circular pipe are related by the expression

$$v_{max} = 1.24V \tag{7.11}$$

Now it is reasonable to assume that the velocity profile can be expressed as a function of the distance from a boundary. Thus

$$v = v_{max} \left(\frac{y}{a}\right)^n \tag{7.12}$$

where y = distance from boundary
a = const ($D/2$ for a pipe)

or
$$v = 1.24V \left(\frac{y}{a}\right)^n \tag{7.13}$$

Blasius showed experimentally that the shear stress in a turbulently flowing fluid within a circular pipe could be expressed nondimensionally in terms of the Reynolds number as

$$\frac{\tau}{\rho V^2} = 0.0395 N_R^{-\frac{1}{4}} \tag{7.14}$$

Rearranging this relationship and substituting Eq. (7·13) gives

$$\tau = 0.0395\rho V^2 \left(\frac{VD}{\nu}\right)^{-\frac{1}{4}}$$

$$= 0.0395\rho D^{-\frac{1}{4}}\nu^{\frac{1}{4}}V^{\frac{7}{4}}$$

$$= 0.0395\rho D^{-\frac{1}{4}}\nu^{\frac{1}{4}}\left[\frac{v}{1.24}\left(\frac{a}{y}\right)^n\right]^{\frac{7}{4}}$$

$$= 0.0395\rho D^{-\frac{1}{4}}\nu^{\frac{1}{4}}\left[\frac{v}{1.24}\left(\frac{D}{2y}\right)^n\right]^{\frac{7}{4}}$$

since $a = D/2$. Now close to the wall τ must be independent of D. Therefore

$$\frac{7n}{4} - \frac{1}{4} = 0$$

or

$$n = \frac{1}{7}$$

Equation (7·13) can now be written as

$$v = 1.24V \left(\frac{y}{a}\right)^{\frac{1}{7}} \tag{7·15}$$

average velocity

which is called the *seventh root law*. It is found to hold true for most of the flow within a circular pipe, breaking down close to the walls where the laminar sublayer exists. This part of the profile can be approximated with a straight line joining the origin to the seventh root profile.

7·6   Fluid resistance to turbulent flow through circular pipes

The most important viscous problem facing the hydraulic engineer concerned with viscous flow through pipes is that of *turbulent* flow through *circular* pipes. Flows through conduits other than circular do take place occasionally, but their comparative rarity and the complexity of the analysis are such that these flows will not be dealt with in this elementary text.

The equation for head loss due to friction in laminar pipe flow was established as

$$h = \frac{32\mu VL}{\gamma D^2} \tag{7·10}$$

h = head loss

and since this has units of feet, it can be rewritten in terms of the velocity head $V^2/2g$. Thus

$$h = \frac{64\mu L g}{\gamma D^2 V} \frac{V^2}{2g}$$

$$= \frac{64\mu L}{\rho V D^2} \frac{V^2}{2g}$$

$$= \frac{64\mu}{\rho V D} \frac{L}{D} \frac{V^2}{2g}$$

$$= \frac{64}{N_R} \frac{L}{D} \frac{V^2}{2g} \qquad (7\cdot16)$$

From Eq. (7·16), assuming the turbulent resistance loss to be similarly related to the velocity head and the pipe length/diameter ratio, Darcy and Weisbach established experimentally the general equation for head loss due to turbulent friction as

$$h = f \frac{L}{D} \frac{V^2}{2g} \qquad (7\cdot17)$$

which is called the *Darcy-Weisbach equation*. The quantity f is called the friction factor and was established experimentally by Darcy and Weisbach for various pipe flows. In laminar flow the friction factor was found to be given by $64/N_R$, as indicated by Eqs. (7·16) and (7·17). In turbulent flows, however, when the surface roughness affects the viscous resistance, the friction factor was found to be a function of both the Reynolds number and the surface roughness e, which is a measure of the height of a typical surface irregularity.

Table 7·1 gives the approximate values for e for several common materials, when new.

Table 7·1   Surface roughness factors

Material	Surface Roughness e, in.
Glass	Smooth
Brass	Smooth
Copper	Smooth
Wrought iron	0.002
Steel	0.002
Galvanized iron	0.006
Cast iron	0.01
Concrete, smooth	0.001
Concrete, rough	0.01

In turbulent flow the friction factor is hard to establish with any degree of certainty. If the surface roughness e, as shown in Fig. 7·13, is nondimensionalized by dividing by the pipe diameter, the friction factor may be read from the experimental results plotted in Fig. 7·14.

As a pipe ages, the surface roughness changes according to the usage received, the fluid flowing, the environment, etc., with the result that

Fig. 7·13.   Surface roughness.

it is impossible to forecast the pipe roughness within an old pipe, except by experience with the local conditions and by inspired guesswork.

Example: Water is siphoned over a 10-ft-high obstruction through a 6-in. galvanized iron pipe with a total length of 200 ft. If the maximum height occurs at the midpoint of the pipe length and the velocity of the water is 10 fps, calculate the vertical distance between the inlet and outlet and the pressure at the highest point in the pipe.

The flow Reynolds number is $\rho V D/\mu = 4.61 \times 10^5$ and so the flow is turbulent.

From Table 7·1, the value of e for galvanized iron is 0.006 in. Hence

$$\frac{e}{D} = \frac{0.006}{6} = 0.001$$

From Fig. 7·14

$$f = 0.0208$$

and therefore, from Eq. (7·17),

$$h = 0.0208 \frac{200}{\frac{1}{2}} \frac{100}{64.4} = 12.9 \text{ ft}$$

Hence, to ensure siphoning, the outlet should be 13 ft lower than the inlet.

Now since the pressure is zero at the outlet, the *ideal* pressure at the highest point would be

$$-(10 + 13) \text{ ft of water} = -23 \text{ ft of water}$$

But since half the friction loss occurs before the highest point and half afterward, the actual pressure at the highest point will be

$$-23 + 13\frac{1}{2} = -16.5 \text{ ft of water}$$
$$= -7.15 \text{ psig}$$

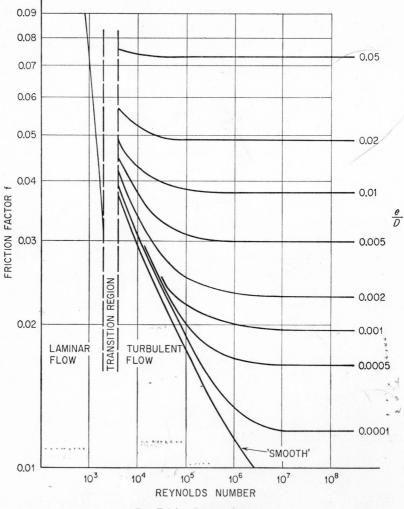

Fig. 7·14. Friction factors.

7·7 Viscous losses due to pipe obstructions

The various head losses that occur because of pipe obstructions may be expressed as a simple function of the flow velocity head, or in the case where the velocity changes, as a function of the head loss. Thus

$$h = k \frac{V^2}{2g} \qquad \text{or} \qquad h = k \frac{V_1^2 - V_2^2}{2g} \qquad (7·18)$$

where k is a constant for the type of obstruction under consideration. The *exact* values of k must be established experimentally, but good approximations for the most commonly occurring obstructions are shown in Table 7·2.

Table 7·2   Loss coefficients for various pipe obstructions

Obstruction Type	k
Sudden enlargement	$\left(1 - \dfrac{A_1}{A_2}\right)^2$
Sudden contraction	$\dfrac{1}{2}\left(1 - \dfrac{A_2}{A_1}\right)$
Gradual entrance to pipe	0.05
45° bend	0.5
90° bend	0.9
180° bend	2.0
Globe valve, open	10.0
Gate valve, open	0.2

Example: Calculate the water flow rate from the large reservoir shown in Fig. 7·15. The pipe is smooth copper and has an overall length of 100 ft.

In this system losses are caused by friction, the sudden contraction at entry, two 90° bends, and an open gate valve. Writing these losses as

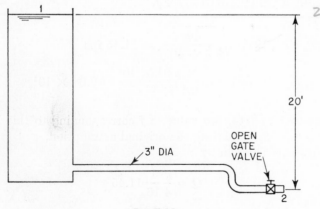

Fig. 7·15

h_L and applying Bernoulli's equation between stations 1 and 2,

$$\frac{p_1}{\gamma} + \frac{V_1{}^2}{2g} + z_1 = \frac{p_2}{\gamma} + \frac{V_2{}^2}{2g} + z_2 + h_L$$

and since $p_1 = p_2 = V_1 = 0$ and $z_1 - z_2 = 20$ ft

$$20 = \frac{V_2{}^2}{2g} + h_L \qquad\qquad (7·19)$$

Now
$$h_L = f \frac{L}{D} \frac{V^2}{2g} + (k_1 + 2k_2 + k_3) \frac{V^2}{2g}$$

where k_1 = const for sudden contraction = 0.5
k_2 = const for 90° elbow = 0.9
k_3 = const for gate valve = 0.2

Therefore
$$h_L = (400f + 0.5 + 1.8 + 0.2) \frac{V^2}{2g}$$

$$= (2.5 + 400f) \frac{V^2}{2g}$$

Substituting this in Eq. (7·19),

$$20 = (3.5 + 400f) \frac{V^2}{2g}$$

Now there are two unknown quantities, f and V. These quantities are related by the curve for smooth pipes of Fig. 7·14, and so a series of approximations must be made to determine values of f and V which will fit both systems. In practice two approximations are usually sufficient.

Assuming a value of 0.0158 for f,

$$V = \sqrt{\frac{40g}{3.5 + 400f}} = 11.45 \text{ fps}$$

and
$$N_R = \frac{11.45 \times 1.94 \times 10^5}{2.1 \times 4} = 2.64 \times 10^5$$

Referring to Fig. 7·14, the value of f corresponding to this Reynolds number is 0.0158, validating the original assumption.

The flow rate is given by

$$Q = \frac{\pi}{4} \frac{1}{16} 11.45$$

$$= 0.56 \text{ cfs}$$

PROBLEMS

(See also Probs. 1·8 to 1·13.)

7·1 Liquid of specific gravity 0.8 flows downward to atmosphere between two vertical glass plates, 2 ft wide and 4 ft long and $\frac{1}{10}$ in. apart, at a rate of 0.08 cfs. If the pressure at the top of the plates is 10 psig, calculate the flow Reynolds number and the fluid viscosity.

7·2 Two pipes 25 ft apart carry water flows in which the pressures are 2.17 psig and 4.76 psig respectively. The high-pressure pipe is 6 ft vertically higher than the low-pressure pipe. Over a 1-ft length the two pipes are connected by two parallel plates 0.05 in. apart. Show that the flow between the two pipes is laminar, and estimate the flow rate between them.

7·3 Lubricating oil of specific gravity 0.9 and viscosity 110×10^{-5} lb-sec/ft^2 flows downward through a vertical tube of 0.197-in. bore at a rate of 0.0012 cfs. If the tube is 3 ft long and open at the lower end, calculate the pressure at the top of the tube and the flow Reynolds number.

7·4 A chemical condenser consists of 40 ft of glass tubing bent into a coil 6 ft in length. The bore of the tubing is 0.15 in., and with the coil in an upright position a fluid of viscosity 4.0×10^{-5} lb-sec/ft^2 and specific gravity 0.9 is fed through by gravity. Calculate the hourly mass flow rate of the fluid.

7·5 Fluid flows from a large reservoir through a horizontal tube 3 ft long and 0.2 in. in bore at a rate of 0.0116 cfs. If the tube is 2 ft below the free surface of the liquid, calculate the flow Reynolds number and the kinematic viscosity of the fluid.

7·6 Water flows through a horizontal 4-in. cast-iron pipe 1,000 ft long with a velocity of 20 fps. Calculate the head loss in the pipe.

7·7 Benzine at 500 psig is pumped through a 40-mile-long 10-in. steel pipe. At the midpoint of the pipe a boost station increases the pressure sufficiently to deliver 9,820 ft^3/hr at atmospheric pressure at the pipe terminal. Estimate the required pressure increase at the boost station.

7·8 Water flows between two reservoirs through a circular concrete duct ($e = 0.03$ in.) with a total length of 300 ft. The duct contains a sudden contraction at entry to a diameter of 6 in., a sudden enlargement at exit, and two 90° bends. Calculate the flow rate when the difference in levels of the reservoirs is 60 ft.

7·9 Water flows from the base of a water tower 100 ft high through a 2-ft cast-iron main with a velocity of 2 fps. At a point 20,000 ft horizontally from the base of the water tower, a 2-in. steel pipe is teed into the main and runs 30 ft vertically upward, ending in a 90° bend and an open globe valve. Calculate the flow rate from the valve.

CHAPTER 8

Open-channel Flow

Open-channel flows occur naturally in the form of rivers and streams, and artificially as canals and other structures which must convey large quantities of fluid.

The flow through such channels is much more complicated in analysis than pipe flow, since the flow area and depth of flow in an open channel are both free to change. Much of the available knowledge of channel flows is empirical in its nature, and the results obtained from it are only approximate. This means that a great deal of caution is advisable when dealing with open-channel flows and that experience is certainly the best teacher.

8·1 The Chézy-Manning equation for uniform flow

When the velocity, cross-sectional area, and depth of a channel flow remain constant from section to section, that flow is said to be uniform. Uniform flows are necessarily steady, but steady flows can be nonuniform, as in the case of a converging or diverging section. Steady flow implies no change of variables with time at a point, but uniform flow implies no change of variables with *time* or *distance*.

In the previous chapter the Darcy-Weisbach equation,

$$h = f \frac{L}{D} \frac{V^2}{2g} \qquad (7 \cdot 17)$$

was established for the flow of fluids through circular pipes. By introducing a new parameter, the hydraulic radius, this equation can be modified for use in flows of a noncircular nature. The hydraulic radius

138

R is defined as

$$R = \frac{flow\ cross\text{-}sectional\ area}{wetted\ perimeter}$$

and for a circular pipe running full,

$$R = \frac{\pi D^2}{4\pi D} = \frac{D}{4}$$

Putting $D = 4R$ in Eq. (7·17) gives

$$h = f\frac{L}{4R}\frac{V^2}{2g}$$

or

$$V = \sqrt{\frac{8ghR}{fL}} \qquad (8\cdot1)$$

Since in open-channel flow the surface pressure is always atmospheric, it follows that any head loss in a uniform flow must appear as a fall in the level of the channel base, so that the ratio h/L in Eq. (8·1) may be replaced by S, the channel slope. Hence

$$V = \sqrt{\frac{8g}{f}}\ \sqrt{RS} = C\sqrt{RS} \qquad (8\cdot2)$$

This is called the *Chézy equation*.

Manning showed that the value of the constant could be approximated as

$$C = \frac{1.5}{n}\ R^{1/6} \qquad (8\cdot3)$$

where *n* is the Manning roughness factor, some typical values for which are shown in Table 8·1.

Table 8·1   Some typical values for Manning roughness factors

Surface Type	Manning Roughness Factor n
Concrete, smooth	0.012
Concrete, rough	0.014
Cast iron	0.015
Natural wood	0.015
Brick	0.017
Rubble or earth	0.025
Gravel	0.035

Thus Eq. (8·2) may be written as

$$V = \frac{1.5}{n} R^{1/6} \sqrt{RS}$$

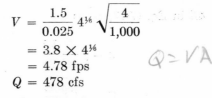

(8·4)

which is called the *Chézy-Manning equation.*

Example: A river with an earthen bed, a flow cross-sectional area of 100 ft², and a hydraulic radius of 4 ft falls 1 ft in 1,000 ft. Calculate the flow rate.

$$V = \frac{1.5}{0.025} 4^{1/6} \sqrt{\frac{4}{1,000}}$$

$$= 3.8 \times 4^{1/6}$$

$$= 4.78 \text{ fps}$$

Hence $Q = 478$ cfs

8·2   Specific energy and critical depth

Consider the steady flow along the channel shown in Fig. 8·1. The total energy per pound at any point is given by

$$\frac{p}{\gamma} + z + \frac{V^2}{2g}$$

and since $p = 0$ in the open surface, this can be expressed as

$$a + y + \frac{V^2}{2g}$$

where a is the height of the stream bed above some horizontal datum and y is the flow depth.

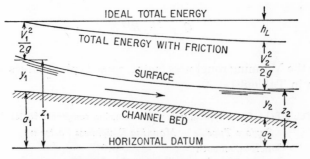

Fig. 8·1.   Flow in an open channel.

The *specific energy* is defined as the distance between the total energy line and the channel bed or

$$E = y + \frac{V^2}{2g}$$

(8·5)

[handwritten annotations in margin: $q = \dfrac{Q\,\text{flow rate}}{\text{width}} = \text{cfs}/\!\!\!/\text{g width of channel.}$ $q = \dfrac{Q}{\text{width}} = c/\!\!\!/\text{lb.}$]

Although the total energy is continually reduced by friction, the specific energy can increase or decrease from section to section. Now if the flow rate per unit channel width is q cfs/ft,

[handwritten: E: energy y: depth]

$$q = yV \qquad\qquad V = \dfrac{q}{y} \tag{8·6}$$

and so

$$E = y + \dfrac{q^2}{2gy^2} \tag{8·7}$$

Putting q as a constant and differentiating Eq. (8·7),

$$\dfrac{dE}{dy} = 1 - \dfrac{q^2}{gy^3} = 0 \qquad \text{when } y = \sqrt[3]{\dfrac{q^2}{g}}$$

which corresponds to a minimum value for E. Equation (8·7) is shown plotted in Fig. 8·2. Since q was assumed as a constant for the flow, the

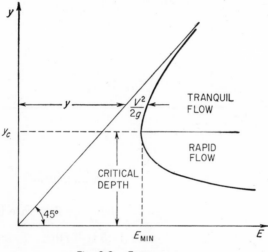

Fig. 8·2. Energy curve.

point of minimum energy corresponds to the point of maximum flow rate per unit energy and is called the critical point. The depth of flow at this point is called the *critical depth* and was found above as

[handwritten: $y_c =$ critical depth]

$$y_c = \sqrt[3]{\dfrac{q^2}{g}} \tag{8·8}$$

[handwritten: $q =$ flow rate]

which is dependent only on the flow rate q.

From Fig. 8·2 it can be seen that at any other value for E there are two possible flow depths to pass the same flow, one deep and one shallow, so that one of these flows is rapid and the other tranquil. These are sometimes referred to as supercritical and subcritical respectively.

y_c critical depth (handwritten annotation)

At the critical depth $= \frac{2}{3} E_{min}$. (handwritten)

$$y_c^3 = \frac{q^2}{g} = (E_{min} - y_c)2y_c^2$$

from Eq. (8·7). Therefore

$$y_c^3 = 2E_{min}y_c^2 - 2y_c^3$$

So
$$3y_c^3 = 2E_{min}y_c^2$$

or
$$y_c = \tfrac{2}{3}E_{min} \qquad \tfrac{2}{3} \text{ minimum Energy (handwritten)}$$

(8·9)

Example: 1,200 cfs of water flows through a rectangular channel 10 ft wide at a depth of 6 ft. Is the flow rapid or tranquil? Determine the specific energy of the flow and the minimum specific energy for the same flow rate.

$$q = \frac{1,200}{10} = 120 \text{ cfs/ft}$$

Therefore
$$y_c = \sqrt[3]{\frac{120^2}{32.2}} = 7.65 \text{ ft}$$

and since 6 is less than 7.65, the flow is rapid.

The flow specific energy is

$$E = y + \frac{q^2}{2gy^2}$$

$$= 6 + \frac{400}{64.4} = 12.2 \text{ ft-lb/lb}$$

and the minimum specific energy for the same flow rate is

$$E_{min} = \tfrac{3}{2}y_c = 11.5 \text{ ft-lb/lb}$$

8·3 Critical depth as a means of flow measurement

From Eq. (8·8) the flow rate per unit channel width can be written as

$$q = \sqrt{gy_c^3}$$

so that if a critical flow can be established, the flow rate may be estimated by knowing only the flow depth.

Consider the flow from a source of constant head over a high, broad horizontal weir, as shown in Fig. 8·3. The specific energy of the flow over the weir is constant and equal to H, whatever the position of the control gate, and the maximum flow rate occurs when the gate is clear of the flow. Since the specific energy is constant, *this maximum flow rate must be critical;* thus it is only necessary to measure the flow depth over such a weir in order to establish the flow rate.

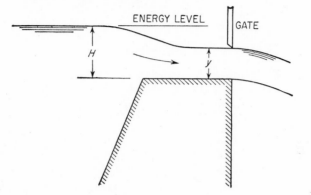

Fig. 8·3.   Flow over a broad weir.

8·4   The hydraulic jump

In Art. 8·2 it was shown that at a specific energy level greater than the minimum there are two possible flow types, rapid and tranquil. The rapid flow case is an unstable one, and under the right conditions it will change suddenly to tranquil flow by means of a hydraulic jump, as shown in Fig. 8·4. This hydraulic jump is analogous to the shock wave of compressible flow.

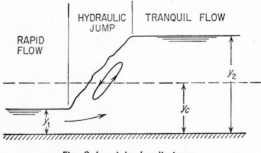

Fig. 8·4.   A hydraulic jump.

Ahead of the hydraulic jump the flow is rapid and the flow depth less than critical; downstream of it the flow is tranquil and deeper than critical. At the jump itself, the surface is turbulent and eddying, with a certain amount of air entrainment. Thus the hydraulic jump is a useful device for flow mixing, preventing sedimentation, and preventing channel erosion since it causes the flow to decelerate.

The depth before and after the jump are related by the expression

$$\frac{q^2}{g} = \frac{y_1 y_2}{2} (y_1 + y_2) \qquad (8\text{-}10)$$

PROBLEMS

8·1   A smooth rectangular concrete channel 10 ft wide and 6 ft deep is to carry 1,000 cfs of water. Calculate the required channel slope.

8·2   An 8-ft-diameter brick sewer with a slope of 2.47×10^{-5} is half full of water. Calculate the flow rate.

8·3   A stream with a gravel bed has a cross-sectional area of 50 ft² and carries a flow of 1,000 cfs. The slope of this stream is 0.008. Calculate the hydraulic radius of the cross section.

8·4   A rectangular channel 12 ft wide passes 600 cfs of water. What is the critical depth of such a flow?

8·5   A flow of 8 fps takes place in a channel 8 ft wide. What is the critical depth for this flow?

8·6   Show that for critical flow the critical depth is given by

$$y_c = \frac{V^2}{g}$$

8·7   10,000 cfs of water passes through a rectangular channel 30 ft wide with a velocity of 30 fps. Is this rapid or tranquil flow? Determine the critical velocity, the specific energy, and the minimum specific energy for this flow rate.

8·8   The flow of a river is passed over a high, broad-crested weir, 8 ft wide. Calculate the flow rate if the depth of water over the weir is 4 ft.

8·9   The top of a high, broad-crested weir is 3 ft below the surface level of a reservoir and well above the level of the discharge channel. Calculate the depth of flow over the weir and the discharge rate.

8·10   A maximum flow rate of 20,500 cfs is to be permitted from a reservoir which is 100 ft deep when full. The flow is controlled by a high, broad-crested weir 200 ft across. What should be the height of this weir above the reservoir bed?

8·11   A flow of 140 cfs flows through a rectangular channel 10 ft wide at a depth of 1 ft. If the flow is rapid, calculate the height of the tranquil flow that would exist after a hydraulic jump.

8·12   The flow of Prob. 8·7 undergoes a hydraulic jump. Calculate the depth of flow after the jump and the specific energy loss due to the jump.

CHAPTER 9

Aircraft in Steady Flight

9·1   The forces and moments acting on an aircraft

Figure 9·1 shows the six possible modes of motion of an aircraft (three translational and three rotational) and the forces and moments acting.

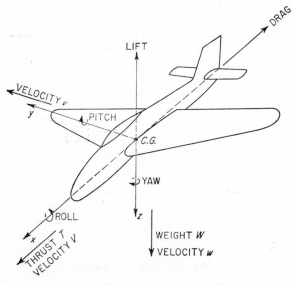

Fig. 9·1.   Definition of axes.

For steady flight under any conditions the net force and moment on the aircraft must obviously be zero, and, so that these forces and moments may be evaluated, it is necessary to adopt a sign convention. The most commonly used system refers to axes that are considered fixed in the aircraft and are called *body axes,* in which x is positive in the forward direction, y is positive to the right or starboard, and z is positive downward. The forces acting in these directions have positive signs. The commonly used notation for the moments is shown in Table 9·1.

Table 9·1   Three-axis rotational convention. Clockwise looking out along each axis

	Roll	Pitch	Yaw
Rotational axis	x	y	z
Moment (lb-ft)	L	M	N
Rate (rad/sec)	p	q	r
Angle	ϕ	θ	β
Positive direction	Starboard wing down	Nose up	Starboard wing back

9·2   The controls and their function

Figure 9·2 shows the external parts of the aircraft which can be moved by the pilot in order to achieve control. These are described below.

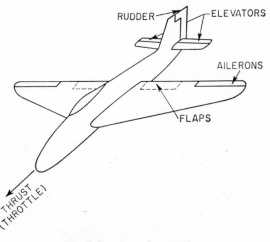

Fig. 9·2.   Aircraft controls.

The ailerons. The outboard trailing edges of the wings, which are connected to the main wing by a hinged support as shown in Fig. 9·3, are called ailerons. They are arranged to move differentially so that one moves up while the other moves down. The lift of the wing with a raised aileron is reduced while the lift of the wing with a depressed aileron is increased, resulting in a rolling moment. Since the aircraft offers a very large resistance to rolling, it is necessary to place the ailerons as far outboard as possible so that the maximum rolling moment may be obtained from them.

The pilot moves the ailerons by moving a control column mounted in the cockpit floor to the left to cause a roll to the left or to the right to cause a roll to the right. In larger aircraft this motion is caused by rotating a small wheel rather like half an automobile steering wheel.

The elevators. The elevators are mounted in the tail-plane trailing edge and are similar to the ailerons, except that they move together. The action of the elevators controls the attitude of the aircraft and this, together with the throttle, controls the aircraft's speed. Since the effect of the tail-plane and elevators is to produce a balancing pitching moment, the effectiveness of the combination is a direct function of the distance of the tail-plane from the center of gravity.

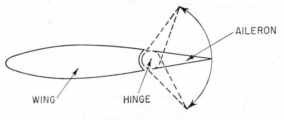

Fig. 9·3.   An aileron.

Movement of the elevators is caused by a fore and aft movement of the control column and is arranged so that pulling back on the control column lifts the aircraft's nose.

In some modern delta-winged aircraft the function of the elevators and ailerons is combined into one control mounted at the trailing edge of the wing and called *elevons*.

The rudder. The rear portion of the tail fin is hinged to form a rudder, movement of which causes the nose of the aircraft to swing to the left or right. The movement is caused by the pilot pressing with his feet against two rudder pedals and is arranged so that moving the left pedal forward moves the aircraft's nose to the left and vice versa. In many nosewheeled aircraft, rudder pedal movement is also connected to a nosewheel steering device for taxiing purposes.

The throttle. The power output from an aircraft engine is controlled by a hand throttle (one per engine), with a friction hold so that once set the throttle position remains constant without further attention. The throttle controls the power output of the engine and hence the behavior of the aircraft. Opening the throttle from a steady flight position will *cause the aircraft to climb,* not to accelerate, unless the elevator position is changed as well.

The flaps. In order to reduce the minimum flying speed to its lowest value for the purpose of taking off and landing, most aircraft wings are fitted with flaps. These are deflected downward into the airstream from the lower side of the wings, which increases the lift and drag of the wing, thus enabling the aircraft to fly at a reduced airspeed and, incidentally, acting as an airbrake. At other times the flaps are retracted into the wing to form a part of it.

Of the many types of flap in use, the two most common are the plain split flap and the Fowler flap, shown in Fig. 9·4a and b respectively. The Fowler flap, although mechanically more complicated, serves to

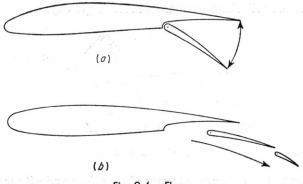

(a)

(b)

Fig. 9·4. Flaps.

increase the wing chord as well as deflect the airstream, thus producing a greater lift than the plain split flap.

9·3   Lift and the wings

Equation (6·7) showed that the force acting on a moving body immersed in a fluid could be expressed as

$$F = C_F \tfrac{1}{2}\rho V^2 L^2 \tag{6·7}$$

and so lift can be written as

$$L = C_L \tfrac{1}{2}\rho V^2 S \tag{9·1}$$

where C_L = lift coefficient
$\qquad S$ = wing area, ft^2
$\qquad L$ = lift = weight in level flight

This lift force, which supports the aircraft in flight, is generated on the wings that have an airfoil section as shown in Fig. 9·5. The line joining the nose of the airfoil to the trailing edge is called the chord line, and the angle between this line and the wind direction is called the angle of attack α. It will be noticed that the wing is not drawn symmetrically about the chord line, but about a line called the camber line, which is curved above the chord line. The maximum distance between

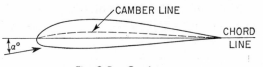

Fig. 9·5. Camber.

these two lines, expressed as a percentage of the chord, is called the camber. The amount of camber varies from airfoil to airfoil, but is generally greatest on slow-speed, high-lift wings, and often zero on high-speed wings.

In flowing around the airfoil, the air passing over the top surface is accelerated while that flowing over the lower surface is decelerated, resulting in a low-pressure region above the wing and a high-pressure region below it, as shown in Fig. 9·6. Obviously, increasing the angle of

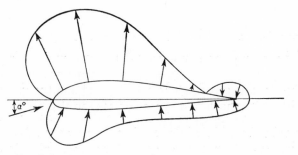

Fig. 9·6.   Pressure distribution round a lifting airfoil.

attack will increase the lift on the wing, and a plot of C_L against α yields a line that is almost straight for conventional wings up to angles of 16–20°, at which value stalling occurs with flow breakaway from the top surface. Figure 9·7 shows a typical C_L-α curve for a cambered section, some interesting features of which should be noted.

  1. At zero angle of attack a small lift remains due to the camber of the section. If the camber is zero, the curve will pass through the origin.

2. The slope of the line, $dC_L/d\alpha$, is theoretically equal to 2π per radian, but in practice is less than this. A value of 4.5 per radian would be typical.

3. The onset of a stall can be gradual or sudden; sharp-edged wings often have severe stalling characteristics.

A certain amount of warning in the form of buffeting is desirable because it serves to warn the pilot that he is flying dangerously close to the stalling point. If a stall does occur, the aircraft is likely to drop suddenly or even begin to spin.

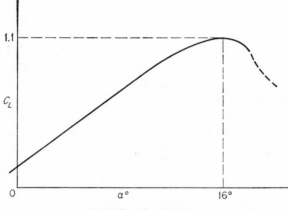

Fig. 9·7. C_L against α.

Example: An aircraft weighing 50,000 lb has a wing area of 1,000 ft^2 and a maximum lift coefficient of 1.4 with flaps down. If the value of the lift coefficient at zero angle of attack is 0.4 and the value of $dC_L/d\alpha$ is 4 per radian with the flaps down, calculate the aircraft's landing speed and the angle of attack when landing.

From Eq. (9·1)

$$V_{\min} = \sqrt{\frac{2L}{\rho S C_{L_{\max}}}}$$

$$= \sqrt{\frac{100,000}{1.4 \times 1,000 \times 0.00238}}$$

since ρ at sea level is 0.00238 slug/ft^3. Therefore

$$V_{\min} = 173 \text{ fps}$$
$$= 118 \text{ mph}$$

Now $dC_L/d\alpha = 4$; therefore

$$\frac{1.4 - 0.4}{\alpha} = 4$$

or $$\alpha = \tfrac{1}{4} \text{ radian} = 14.3°$$

9·4 Drag

The drag force on an aircraft is expressed in terms of a total drag coefficient; thus

$$D = C_D \tfrac{1}{2}\rho V^2 S \tag{9·2}$$

where C_D = total drag coefficient
   D = total drag = thrust in level flight

Unlike the lift, the drag is composed of many parts which may be summarized as follows:

1. The *extra to wing drag*, which includes the drag of the entire aircraft with the exception of the wings
2. The *wing profile drag*, which is the drag of the wings alone, while generating no lift
3. The *induced drag*, which is caused by the wing producing lift

The first two of these are added together to give the total profile or parasite drag, as shown in the drag break-down outlined in Fig. 9·8.

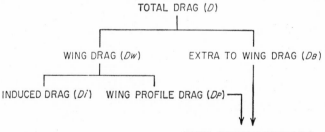

TOTAL DRAG (D)

WING DRAG (D_W)   EXTRA TO WING DRAG (D_B)

INDUCED DRAG (D_i)   WING PROFILE DRAG (D_P)

TOTAL PROFILE DRAG (D_z)

Fig. 9·8. Drag breakdown.

Assigning coefficients to these drags so that

$$C_D = C_{D_i} + C_{D_z} \tag{9·3}$$

where C_{D_i} = induced drag coefficient
   C_{D_z} = profile drag coefficient

shows the reason for this grouping of the drags. The profile drag coefficient remains nearly constant with incidence, whereas the induced drag coefficient varies considerably. A plot of C_D against $C_L{}^2$ is shown in Fig. 9·9 and is found to be nearly straight, with a slope of $k/\pi A$, where k

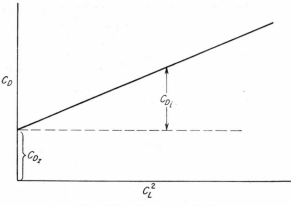

Fig. 9·9. C_D against $C_L{}^2$.

is the induced drag factor (ideally equal to 1, but in practice between 1 and 2) and A is the aspect ratio of the wing.

$$A = \frac{\text{span}}{\text{mean chord}} = \frac{2s}{\bar{c}} \qquad\qquad (9\cdot4)$$

Thus the total drag coefficient can be written as

$$C_D = C_{D_z} + \frac{k}{\pi A} C_L{}^2 \qquad\qquad (9\cdot5)$$

Now writing the total drag as

$$
\begin{aligned}
D &= C_D \tfrac{1}{2}\rho V^2 S \\
  &= \tfrac{1}{2}\rho V^2 S \left(C_{D_z} + \frac{k}{\pi A} C_L{}^2 \right) \\
  &= \tfrac{1}{2}\rho V^2 S \left[C_{D_z} + \frac{k}{\pi A} \left(\frac{L}{\tfrac{1}{2}\rho V^2 S} \right)^2 \right] \\
  &= aV^2 + \frac{b}{V^2} \qquad\qquad (9\cdot6)
\end{aligned}
$$

where a and b are constants, it can be seen that the profile drag varies as the velocity squared, whereas the induced drag varies inversely as the velocity squared. Plotting these as shown in Fig. 9·10 indicates that there is a minimum drag speed; and since the power is given by

$$P = DV = aV^3 + \frac{b}{V} \tag{9·7}$$

there will also be a minimum power required speed.

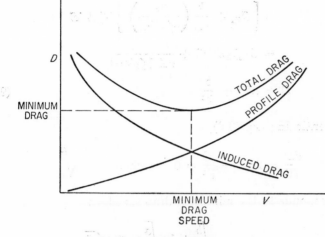

Fig. 9·10. Drag against speed.

Example: Given these additional data for the aircraft of the example to Art. 9·3, calculate the horsepower required for flight at a speed of 300 mph at sea level.

$$C_{D_i} = 0.03 \qquad k = 1.5 \qquad A = 16$$

$$C_L = \frac{2 \times 50,000 \times 60^2}{0.00238 \times 1,000 \times (300 \times 88)^2} = 0.217$$

and therefore

$$C_D = 0.03 + \frac{1.5}{16\pi}(0.217)^2 = 0.0314$$

Hence
$$D = \tfrac{1}{2} \times 0.00238 \times 440^2 \times 1,000 \times 0.0314$$
$$= 7,280 \text{ lb}$$

and the required horsepower is

$$\frac{DV}{550} = \frac{7,280 \times 440}{550} = 5,820 \text{ hp}$$

9·5 Steady, straight, and level flight

For level flight the moments L, M, and N are zero and the thrust and drag are equal, as are the lift and weight. Therefore

$$L = W = C_L \tfrac{1}{2}\rho V^2 S$$

$$D = T = \left(C_{D_s} + \frac{k}{\pi A} C_L{}^2 \right) \tfrac{1}{2}\rho V^2 S$$

$$= \left[C_{D_s} + \frac{k}{\pi A} \left(\frac{W}{\tfrac{1}{2}\rho V^2 S} \right)^2 \right] \tfrac{1}{2}\rho V^2 S$$

$$= C_{D_s} \tfrac{1}{2}\rho V^2 S + \frac{k}{\pi A} \frac{W^2}{\tfrac{1}{2}\rho V^2 S} \tag{9·8}$$

$$D = aV^2 + \frac{b}{V^2} \tag{9·6}$$

Now differentiating Eq. (9·6),

$$\frac{dD}{dV} = 2aV - \frac{2b}{V^3} = 0 \qquad \text{when } V = \sqrt[4]{\frac{b}{a}} \tag{9·9}$$

which corresponds to the minimum drag speed, so

$$D_{\min} = a\sqrt{\frac{b}{a}} + b\sqrt{\frac{a}{b}} = 2\sqrt{ab} \tag{9·10}$$

and this corresponds to equal profile and induced drags. Now from Eq. (9·8)

$$D_{\min} = 2\sqrt{\tfrac{1}{2}\rho S C_{D_s} \frac{2kW^2}{\pi A \rho S}} = 2W\sqrt{\frac{kC_{D_s}}{\pi A}} \tag{9·11}$$

and
$$V_{md} = \sqrt[4]{\frac{2kW^2}{\pi A \rho S} \frac{2}{\rho S C_{D_s}}} = \sqrt[4]{\frac{4kW^2}{\pi A C_{D_s}\rho^2 S^2}} \tag{9·12}$$

It is interesting to note from Eq. (9·11) that the value of the minimum drag is independent of altitude, but from Eq. (9·12) that the value of the minimum drag speed rises with increase in altitude.

Example: Calculate the minimum drag and the minimum drag speed for the aircraft of the two previous examples when at sea level.

$$D_{\min} = 2 \times 50{,}000 \sqrt{\frac{1.5 \times 0.03}{16\pi}} = 2{,}960 \text{ lb}$$

and
$$V_{md} = \sqrt[4]{\frac{4 \times 1.5 \times 50,000^2}{\pi \times 16 \times 0.03 \times (0.00238 \times 1,000)^2}}$$
$$= 204 \text{ fps}$$
$$= 139 \text{ mph}$$

9·6 Steady gliding flight

In gliding flight the drag force is overcome by a component of the weight, and so the aircraft must descend. Figure 9·11 shows the forces acting on an aircraft in a shallow glide of angle θ to the horizontal.

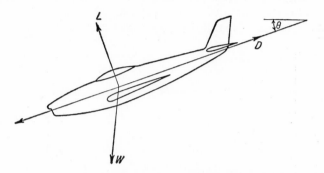

Fig. 9·11. An aircraft in a steady glide.

Resolving forces in the directions of the lift and drag,
$$L = W \cos \theta$$
$$D = W \sin \theta$$
and therefore
$$\frac{L}{D} = \cot \theta \qquad\qquad (9·13)$$

The ratio L/D is called the lift/drag ratio and occurs often in aircraft performance work. The minimum gliding angle, which gives the maximum horizontal distance for a given altitude loss, corresponds to a maximum value of L/D.

Example: A sailplane with a maximum lift/drag ratio of 18 at a forward speed of 40 fps meets a thermal updraft of 3.5 fps. Is the sailplane able to soar in such an updraft?

The best gliding angle is given by
$$\cot \theta = 18$$
therefore
$$\theta = 3.15°$$

The rate of sink of the sailplane is then

$$40 \sin 3.15° = 2.2 \text{ fps}$$

and since the updraft is greater than this, the sailplane can soar.

9·7 Steady climbing flight

There are two basic cases to consider here, the shallow climb case with the aircraft substantially horizontal and the steep climb case with the aircraft inclined to the horizon.

The shallow climb. Since for this case the aircraft is considered horizontal, the lift and weight are equal, as are the thrust and drag. A plot of power required to maintain level flight against speed is shown in

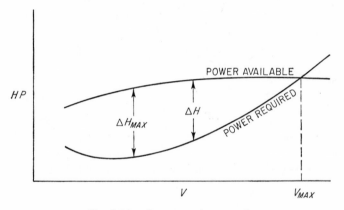

Fig. 9·12.   Power against speed.

Fig. 9·12, with a typical power available curve superimposed. The point at which these two curves cross represents the maximum flight speed, and at all other velocities the difference between the lines ΔH is the amount of power available for climbing. Therefore, if v is the vertical rate of climb,

$$\Delta H = \frac{Wv}{550}$$

or

$$v = \frac{550 \, \Delta H}{W} \text{ fps}$$

and

$$v = \frac{33,000 \, \Delta H}{W} \text{ fpm} \tag{9·14}$$

The steep climb. Consider the case of the same aircraft climbing steeply at angle θ to the horizon as shown in Fig. 9·13, but at the same angle of attack and hence the same C_L. Since the required lift decreases with increase in climb angle, it is apparent that the climbing speed is less than for the level-flight case. Referring to the climbing case with

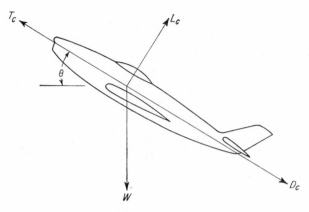

Fig. 9·13. A steeply climbing aircraft.

the suffix c and the level-flight case without suffix,

$$L_c = W \cos \theta = C_L \tfrac{1}{2} \rho V_c^2 S$$

and
$$L = W = C_L \tfrac{1}{2} \rho V^2 S$$

Hence
$$\cos \theta = \left(\frac{V_c}{V}\right)^2$$

or
$$V_c = V \sqrt{\cos \theta} \tag{9·15}$$

Now resolving the forces in the direction of thrust,

$$T_c = D_c + W \sin \theta$$
$$= D_c \left(1 + \frac{W}{D_c} \sin \theta\right)$$

but $D_c = C_D \tfrac{1}{2} \rho V_c^2 S$ and $D = C_D \tfrac{1}{2} \rho V^2 S$. Therefore

$$D_c = D \left(\frac{V_c}{V}\right)^2 = D \cos \theta$$

and so
$$T_c = D \cos \theta \left(1 + \frac{W \sin \theta}{D \cos \theta}\right)$$
$$= D \cos \theta \left(1 + \frac{L}{D} \tan \theta\right)$$

since $W = L$ for the level-flight case; and since in level flight $T = D$,

$$\frac{T_c}{T} = \cos \theta \left(1 + \frac{L}{D} \tan \theta \right) \tag{9·16}$$

Equation (9·16) makes it possible to determine the climbing thrust required, provided that the angle of attack is known so that the lift/drag ratio may be estimated for that particular angle.

The power required in climbing is

$$H_c = \frac{T_c V_c}{550} = \frac{D \cos \theta}{550} \left(1 + \frac{L}{D} \tan \theta \right) V \sqrt{\cos \theta}$$
$$= \frac{DV}{550} \cos^{3/2} \theta \left(1 + \frac{L}{D} \tan \theta \right)$$

and since $DV/550$ is the level-flight power requirement,

$$\frac{H_c}{H} = \cos^{3/2} \theta \left(1 + \frac{L}{D} \tan \theta \right) \tag{9·17}$$

Example: A fighter aircraft with a weight of 30,000 lb requires 2,000 hp to fly at 300 mph in straight and level flight. At what speed and with what power may the aircraft be climbed at an angle of 45°?

The drag in level flight is

$$\frac{2{,}000 \times 550}{440} = 2{,}500 \text{ lb}$$

and thus the lift/drag ratio is

$$\frac{30{,}000}{2{,}500} = 12$$

The climbing power required is

$$H_c = 2{,}000 \times 0.594(1 + 12)$$
$$= 15{,}500 \text{ hp}$$

and the climbing velocity is

$$V_c = 300 \sqrt{\cos 45°} = 252 \text{ mph}$$

9·8 Steady banked turns

Figure 9·14 shows an aircraft in a steady turn of radius R ft. The aircraft is banked through an angle of $\phi°$ so that a component of the lift force can balance the centrifugal force WV^2/gR acting out of the turn.

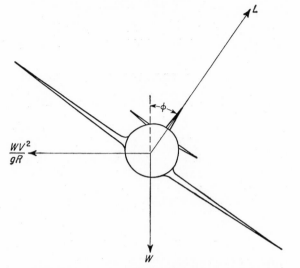

Fig. 9·14.   An aircraft in a steady banked turn.

Resolving the forces vertically and horizontally,

$$L \cos \phi = W$$

$$L \sin \phi = \frac{WV^2}{gR}$$

Hence

$$\tan \phi = \frac{V^2}{gR} \qquad (9·18)$$

and

$$\sec \phi = \frac{L}{W} \qquad (9·19)$$

Example: An aircraft with a maximum lift of three times its weight flies in a level banked turn. Calculate the minimum radius of the turn and the required bank angle when the aircraft is flying at a speed of 400 mph.

From Eq. (9·18) it can be seen that for R to be a minimum, ϕ must be a maximum; hence L/W must be a maximum. Thus

$$\sec \phi = \frac{3W}{W} = 3$$

or

$$\phi = 70.6°$$

and so
$$R = \frac{V^2}{g \tan \phi}$$
$$= \frac{(400 \times {}^{88}\!/\!_{60})^2}{32.2 \times 2.84} = 3{,}770 \text{ ft}$$

PROBLEMS

The following problems refer to an aircraft with these data:

Weight	50,000 lb	Span	100 ft
C_{D_z}	0.05	Mean chord	8 ft
$C_{L_{\max}}$ (no flap)	1.3	Available hp	$400\sigma \sqrt{V}$, where V
$C_{L_{\max}}$ (with flap)	2.0	is the forward speed in fps and σ is
Induced drag factor	1.2	the ratio of density to sea-level
		value for density.

9·1 Determine the minimum drag speed, the minimum drag, the landing speed (with full flap), the stalling speed, and the best gliding angle at altitudes of 0, 10,000, 20,000, and 30,000 ft.

9·2 Plot curves of drag against speed for each of the above altitudes and comment on the results. Mark the values calculated in Prob. 9·1 on the curves.

9·3 Plot required power and available power against speed separately for each altitude. From these plots determine: (*a*) the maximum level speed; (*b*) the maximum rate of climb; (*c*) the best climbing speed for each altitude. Mark the stalling speed with and without flaps on each curve. Comment on the results.

9·4 Plot the maximum rate of climb against altitude and extrapolate to estimate the aircraft's ceiling. Taking 2,000-ft intervals along this curve, determine the time required to climb to 20,000 ft.

9·5 What is the steepest climb angle that this aircraft can achieve at sea level, and at what speed? If a rocket assist were available, how much thrust would be needed to increase the climb angle to 20° at the same speed?

9·6 Calculate the required bank angle and the radius of the smallest turn that the aircraft can make at 300 fps at sea level.

CHAPTER 10

Longitudinal Control and Stability

In order to study the stability of an airplane, it is necessary to understand the effects of each component on the stability. The various parts will be considered separately and several new parameters will be introduced so that the last section of this chapter may be easily understood.

10·1 The longitudinal stability of a wing alone

The forces acting on a lifting wing can be summarized as the weight, acting through the center of gravity; the lift, acting through a point known as the aerodynamic center; and a pitching moment about this point, as shown in Fig. 10·1. The aerodynamic center is a point on the

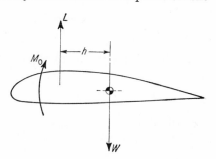

Fig. 10·1. Forces acting on a lifting wing.

wing about which an increase of lift causes no change of pitching moment; or alternatively, it is the point at which increments of lift may be considered to act. For most conventional wings, this point coincides with the quarter chord point.

In coefficient form the total pitching moment about the center of gravity can be expressed as

$$M = C_m \tfrac{1}{2}\rho V^2 S \bar{c} \qquad (10·1)$$

where $\bar{c}$ is the wing mean chord (note that it is necessary to include this extra length dimension in order to achieve units of moment) and the pitching moment coefficient about the aerodynamic center is denoted by C_{m_0}. Since the aerodynamic center has been defined as the point about which no change of pitching moment occurs with an increase of lift, it follows that C_{m_0} is a constant for each wing, although C_m, the moment coefficient about the center of gravity, changes with angle of attack.

If a wing in steady flight is disturbed from its equilibrium position by a gust, so that it tips nose up, a negative or nose down moment is necessary to restore the wing to its original position. It then becomes

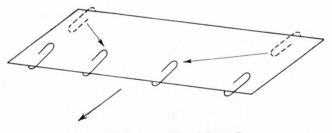

Fig. 10·2.   A stabilized "wing."

apparent that the rate of change of pitching moment coefficient with angle of attack must be negative for stability or

$$\frac{dC_m}{d\alpha} < 0 \qquad \text{for stability} \tag{10·2}$$

Taking moments about the center of gravity in Fig. 10·1,

$$M = M_0 + hL$$

or
$$C_m \tfrac{1}{2}\rho V^2 S\bar{c} = C_{m_0}\tfrac{1}{2}\rho V^2 S\bar{c} + hC_L\tfrac{1}{2}\rho V^2 S$$

and dividing by $\tfrac{1}{2}\rho V^2 S\bar{c}$,

$$C_m = C_{m_0} + \frac{h}{\bar{c}} C_L$$

Differentiating this with respect to α,

$$\frac{dC_m}{d\alpha} = \frac{h}{\bar{c}} \frac{dC_L}{d\alpha} \tag{10·3}$$

since C_{m_0} is a constant. Now since $dC_L/d\alpha$ is positive, it follows that h must be negative for stability. Or, in other words, *the center of gravity must be ahead of the aerodynamic center*. This can easily be demonstrated by fastening four paper clips to the corners of a narrow sheet of card-board. When launched, the cardboard will tumble owing to its instability. However, moving the two rear paper clips to the leading edge, as shown in Fig. 10·2, will stabilize the "wing" if the clips are heavy enough, and the cardboard will fly in a stable condition, at least until it stalls.

Example: A model flying wing has a weight of 2 lb and a c.g. at $0.3\bar{c}$. What is the minimum weight that will cause stability when attached to the nose?

If the minimum weight is w, taking moments about the trailing edge must yield a new c.g. at the quarter chord point for marginal stability. Therefore

$$w\bar{c} + 2 \times 0.7\bar{c} = (2 + w)0.75\bar{c}$$
$$w + 1.4 = 1.5 + 0.75w$$

or
$$w = 0.4 \text{ lb}$$

10·2   The tail volume ratio

The effectiveness of the tail-plane in producing a balancing pitching moment depends upon two variables, the lift of the tail-plane and its distance from the aircraft's center of gravity. Since the lift of the tail-plane is proportional to its area, the tail-plane moment is proportional to the product of the tail-plane area and its distance from the center of gravity, which product has units of volume. Dividing this quantity by a volume that reflects the aircraft size (in this case, the wing area multiplied by the wing chord) gives a dimensionless quantity called the tail volume ratio $\bar{V}$, which is a direct measure of the tail-plane effectiveness. Thus

$$\bar{V} = \frac{S_T l_T}{S\bar{c}} \tag{10·4}$$

where S_T = tail-plane area
l_T = tail-plane moment arm

Example: An aircraft with a wing area of 400 ft² and an aspect ratio of 16 has a tail-plane of 25 ft² mounted with its quarter chord point 40 ft behind the aircraft's c.g. Calculate the tail volume ratio.

$$A = \frac{\text{span}}{\text{chord}} = \frac{\text{area}}{(\text{chord})^2}$$

Therefore
$$\bar{c} = \sqrt{400/16} = 5 \text{ ft}$$

and so
$$\bar{V} = \frac{25 \times 40}{400 \times 5} = 0.5$$

10·3   Downwash and tail-plane incidence

Behind an aircraft wing is a region of disturbance in which there is a downward air movement called the downwash. Since the tail-plane is mounted at the rear of the aircraft in most conventional layouts, it has to act in this region of downwash, which tends to reduce the effective tail-plane angle of attack. Figure 10·3 shows the airflow across a

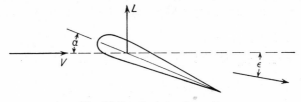

Fig. 10·3.   Downwash angle.

lifting wing with the flow turned through an angle ϵ (epsilon) to cause the downwash. The value of ϵ depends upon the lift the wing is producing and hence upon the angle of attack. The curve of ϵ against α is very much like the C_L-α curve, as can be seen from Fig. 10·4; and its slope, $d\epsilon/d\alpha$, is an important parameter in aircraft stability work. The value of this slope is usually about $\frac{1}{3}$ to $\frac{1}{2}$.

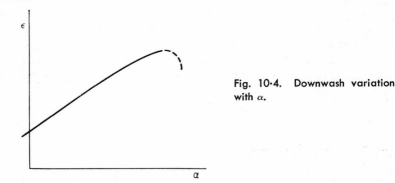

Fig. 10·4.   Downwash variation with α.

If the angle of attack of the aircraft is α and the tail-plane is set on the aircraft at an angle α_T to the wing chord, the effective tail-plane incidence is

$$\alpha_{tp} = \alpha + \alpha_T - \epsilon \tag{10·5}$$

10·4   Tail-plane lift and longitudinal balance

Figure 10·5 shows diagrammatically the forces acting on an aircraft in level flight. Obviously, for balance the total moment about the center of gravity must be zero.

Therefore $$Lh = l_T L_T$$

and so $$L_T = \frac{Lh}{l_T} = \frac{C_L \frac{1}{2}\rho V^2 Sh}{l_T}$$

Writing the tail-plane lift in terms of the tail-plane lift coefficient C_{L_T},

$$C_{L_T}\frac{1}{2}\rho V^2 S_T = \frac{C_L \frac{1}{2}\rho V^2 Sh}{l_T}$$

Hence $$C_{L_T} = \frac{C_L Sh}{S_T l_T} = C_L \frac{h}{\bar{c}} \frac{l}{\bar{V}} \qquad (10\cdot6)$$

It will be observed that if the aircraft's center of gravity is ahead of the aerodynamic center, so that $h/\bar{c}$ is negative, the tail-plane lift

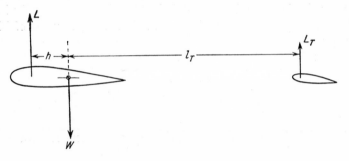

Fig. 10·5.   Longitudinal balance.

coefficient will be negative, and the lift will be directed downward. The tail-plane lift is varied by changing the position of the elevators; and so that this lift may be considered to increase with the increase of elevator angle η (eta), the elevator angle is measured as positive downward, as shown in Fig. 10·6.

Fig. 10·6.   Elevator movement.

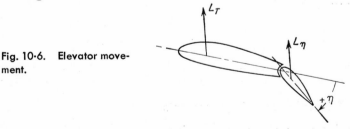

The tail-plane lift coefficient can now be written as

$$C_{L_T} = \frac{dC_{L_T}}{d\alpha}(\alpha + \alpha_T - \epsilon) + \frac{dC_{L_T}}{d\eta}\eta$$

where $\dfrac{dC_{L_T}}{d\alpha}$ = rate of change of tail-plane lift coefficient with angle of

attack = a_1

$\dfrac{dC_{L_T}}{d\eta}$ = rate of change of tail-plane lift coefficient with elevator

angle = a_2

So $\qquad\qquad C_{L_T} = a_1(\alpha + \alpha_T - \epsilon) + a_2\eta$ $\qquad\qquad$ (10·7)

Example: The aircraft of the example of Art. 10·2 has a weight of 20,000 lb and a c.g. at the leading edge of the mean chord. If the values of a_1 and a_2 are 3 per radian and 2.5 per radian respectively and the effective tail-plane angle of attack is 1°, calculate the tail-plane lift coefficient and the necessary elevator angle at a flight speed of 300 mph at sea level.

The overall lift coefficient is

$$C_L = \frac{W}{\tfrac{1}{2}\rho V^2 S} = 0.217$$

and the c.g. is $\tfrac{1}{4}\bar{c}$ ahead of the aerodynamic center, so that

$$\frac{h}{\bar{c}} = -\frac{1}{4}$$

Now from Eq. (10·6)

$$C_{L_T} = 0.217 \times -\frac{1}{4} \times \frac{1}{0.5} = -0.108$$

and from Eq. (10·7)

$$-0.108 = 3\,\frac{1}{57.3} + 2.5\,\frac{1}{57.3}\,\eta$$

Hence $\qquad\qquad \eta = -\dfrac{0.108 \times 57.3 + 3}{2.5} = -3.7°$

10·5 Trim tabs and hinge moments

Consideration of the forces acting on a depressed elevator, as shown in Fig. 10·6, will show that a hinge moment H has to be resisted in order to keep the elevator deflected. In the case of an aircraft with fully powered controls, this hinge moment is resisted by hydraulic pressure and is of no further concern; but in a manually controlled aircraft the pilot has to supply the necessary moment, and so it becomes important to reduce it in order to prevent pilot fatigue. The addition of a second, smaller control moving in the opposite sense to the elevator, as shown in Fig. 10·7, causes a small force to exist with a large moment arm opposing the elevator hinge moment. Such a control is called a tab, and its deflection β is also measured as positive downward.

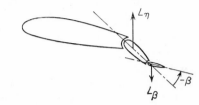

Fig. 10·7. Tab movement.

The hinge moment coefficient is expressed as

$$C_H = b_0 + \frac{dC_H}{d\alpha}\alpha_{tp} + \frac{dC_H}{d\eta}\eta + \frac{dC_H}{d\beta}\beta$$

where b_0 = a constant

$\dfrac{dC_H}{d\alpha}$ = rate of change of hinge moment coefficient with angle of

attack = b_1

$\dfrac{dC_H}{d\eta}$ = rate of change of hinge moment coefficient with elevator

angle = b_2

$\dfrac{dC_H}{d\beta}$ = rate of change of hinge moment coefficient with tab

angle = b_3

Therefore $\qquad C_H = b_0 + b_1\alpha_{tp} + b_2\eta + b_3\beta$ (10·8)

The value of b_0 depends upon the static balance of the elevator. If the leading edge is weighted so that the center of gravity of the control lies at the hinge point, $b_0 = 0$.

The value of b_1 depends upon the position of the control hinge but is generally arranged to be equal to zero. b_2 and b_3 must be negative to prevent overcontrol, which means that if the control is displaced, it must tend to return to its equilibrium position and not travel further from this position.

b_3 can be reduced by the use of horn balancing, as shown in Fig. 10·8. This type of control is arranged so that some of the control surface projects into the airstream well ahead of the hinge to cause a balancing hinge moment.

When the control is arranged so that $b_0 = b_1 = 0$, the hinge moment equals zero when

$$b_2\eta + b_3\beta = 0$$

or
$$\beta = -\frac{b_2}{b_3}\eta \qquad (10.9)$$

Since b_2 and b_3 are both negative, *β and η must have opposite signs.*

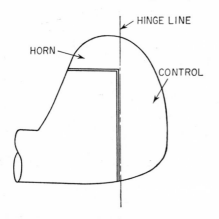

HINGE LINE

HORN

CONTROL

Fig. 10·8.   A horn-balanced control.

10·6   Complete aircraft stability

It was shown in Art. 10·1 that for a wing to be longitudinally stable,

$$\frac{dC_m}{d\alpha} < 0 \qquad (10.2)$$

and this is equally true for a complete aircraft.

Writing the pitching moment about the center of gravity for the entire aircraft shown in Fig. 10·9 as

$$M = M_0 + hL - l_T L_T$$

or in coefficient form, by dividing through by $\frac{1}{2}\rho V^2 S\bar{c}$,

$$C_m = C_{m_0} + \frac{h}{\bar{c}}C_L - C_{L_T}\bar{V}$$

Hence from Eq. (10·7)

$$C_m = C_{m_0} + \frac{h}{\bar{c}} C_L - \bar{V}[a_1(\alpha + \alpha_T - \epsilon) + a_2\eta] \qquad \textbf{(10·10)}$$

Stick fixed stability and stick fixed static margin. For a manually controlled aircraft there are two stability cases to consider—one with the controls rigid, called "stick fixed," and one with the controls free, called "stick free." An aircraft with fully powered controls will always be considered stick fixed.

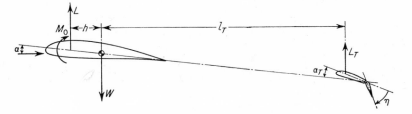

Fig. 10·9. Forces on a complete aircraft.

In the stick fixed case the elevator angle η is constant, and so Eq. (10·10) may be differentiated as

$$\frac{dC_m}{d\alpha} = \frac{h}{\bar{c}}\frac{dC_L}{d\alpha} - \bar{V}a_1\left(1 - \frac{d\epsilon}{d\alpha}\right) \qquad < 0 \text{ for stability} \quad \textbf{(10·11)}$$

since C_{m_0} and α_T are constants.

Dividing Eq. (10·11) by $dC_L/d\alpha$, or a, gives

$$\frac{dC_m}{dC_L} = \frac{h}{\bar{c}} - \bar{V}\frac{a_1}{a}\left(1 - \frac{d\epsilon}{d\alpha}\right) = -h_n \qquad \textbf{(10·12)}$$

where h_n is the "stick fixed static margin," or *the distance of the aircraft's actual center of gravity ahead of the center of gravity position for neutral stability, measured as a fraction of the mean chord with the stick fixed.* The minus sign is introduced in Eq. (10·12) so that an aircraft with positive stability may have a positive static margin.

Stick free stability and stick free static margin. Differentiating Eq. (10·10) and retaining the term in η, since the control is now considered free to move,

$$\frac{dC_m}{d\alpha} = \frac{h}{\bar{c}}\frac{dC_L}{d\alpha} - \bar{V}\left[a_1\left(1 - \frac{d\epsilon}{d\alpha}\right) + a_2\frac{d\eta}{d\alpha}\right] \qquad \textbf{(10·13)}$$

Now the stick free case can best be defined as having zero elevator hinge moment; so, from Eq. (10·8), (neglecting the tab)

$$0 = b_0 + b_1\alpha_{tp} + b_2\eta$$
$$= b_0 + b_1(\alpha + \alpha_T - \epsilon) + b_2\eta$$

Hence
$$\eta = -\frac{b_0}{b_2} - \frac{b_1}{b_2}(\alpha + \alpha_T - \epsilon)$$

and so
$$\frac{d\eta}{d\alpha} = -\frac{b_1}{b_2}\left(1 - \frac{d\epsilon}{d\alpha}\right)$$

Substituting this in Eq. (10·13),

$$\frac{dC_m}{d\alpha} = \frac{h}{\bar{c}}\frac{dC_L}{d\alpha} - \bar{V}\left[a_1\left(1 - \frac{d\epsilon}{d\alpha}\right) - \frac{a_2 b_1}{b_2}\left(1 - \frac{d\epsilon}{d\alpha}\right)\right]$$

$$= \frac{h}{\bar{c}}\frac{dC_L}{d\alpha} - \bar{V}a_1\left(1 - \frac{d\epsilon}{d\alpha}\right)\left(1 - \frac{a_2 b_1}{a_1 b_2}\right) \quad < 0 \text{ for stability} \quad \textbf{(10·14)}$$

Dividing Eq. (10·14) by $dC_L/d\alpha$, or a, gives

$$\frac{dC_m}{d\alpha} = \frac{h}{\bar{c}} - \bar{V}\frac{a_1}{a}\left(1 - \frac{d\epsilon}{d\alpha}\right)\left(1 - \frac{a_2 b_1}{a_1 b_2}\right) = -h'_n \quad \textbf{(10·15)}$$

where h'_n is the "stick free static margin," or *the distance of the actual center of gravity ahead of the neutral point, measured as a fraction of the mean chord with the stick free.*

Example: The aircraft of Art. 10·4 has a lift-curve slope of 4 per radian and values for b_1 and b_2 of 0.1 and -0.3 respectively. If the value of $d\epsilon/d\alpha$ is 0.3, calculate the static margins, stick fixed and stick free, and the distance of the c.g. ahead of the neutral point in each case.

$$h_n = \bar{V}\frac{a_1}{a}\left(1 - \frac{d\epsilon}{d\alpha}\right) - \frac{h}{\bar{c}}$$
$$= 0.5 \times \tfrac{3}{4}(1 - 0.3) + 0.25$$
$$= 0.513$$

Hence the distance of the c.g. ahead of the stick fixed neutral point is
$$0.513\bar{c} = 30.8 \text{ in.}$$

$$h'_n = \bar{V}\frac{a_1}{a}\left(1 - \frac{d\epsilon}{d\alpha}\right)\left(1 - \frac{a_2 b_1}{a_1 b_2}\right) - \frac{h}{\bar{c}}$$
$$= 0.5 \times \tfrac{3}{4}(1 - 0.3)\left(1 + \frac{2.5 \times 0.1}{3.0 \times 0.3}\right) + 0.25$$
$$= 0.587$$

and so, in this case, the distance of the c.g. ahead of the stick free neutral point is

$$0.587\bar{c} = 35.2 \text{ in.}$$

PROBLEMS

The following problems refer to the aircraft of the Chap. 9 problems with this additional information available:

No lift angle of attack = 0°
Tail-plane area = 60 ft²
Distance between c.g. and tail lift = 80 ft
c.g. position (standard) = 2 ft behind quarter chord point

$$a_1 = 3.5 \qquad \frac{C_L}{d\alpha} = 4.0$$
$$a_2 = 2.5$$
$$b_1 = -0.5 \qquad \frac{d\epsilon}{d\alpha} = 0.5$$
$$b_2 = 5.1$$

10·1 Find the tail volume ratio; the static margins, stick fixed and stick free, in terms of the wing chord and in inches; and the neutral point positions. Is this a stable airplane and, if so, which is more stable, stick free or stick fixed?

10·2 The tail plane of the aircraft is a symmetrical section mounted at zero incidence on the fuselage, with a maximum lift coefficient of 0.8 with full elevator. Find the possible extent of c.g. travel ahead of the neutral point, neglecting any contribution of tail-plane lift to the total lift and remembering that the aircraft must be stable in both modes.

10·3 In the course of a flight the c.g. of this aircraft moves forward 18 in. by virtue of the fuel used and redistribution of payload. Calculate the new static margins, stick fixed and stick free. How is the stability affected by this c.g. shift?

10·4 If the landing angle of attack of this aircraft is 25°, determine the necessary elevator angle for landing.

10·5 The wing of the aircraft has zero camber. Calculate the aircraft angle of attack at 250 mph at 10,000 ft and the corresponding elevator angle.

10·6 Draw a one-sixtieth scale drawing of this aircraft and mark on it the positions of the c.g. (standard), the c.g. travel range, the two neutral points, the aerodynamic center, and the two static margins.

The U.S. Standard Atmosphere

Altitude, thousands of ft	Temperature, °F	Pressure, psia	Density, slug/ft³
0	59	14.7	0.00238
5	41.2	12.2	0.00204
10	23.4	10.1	0.001755
15	5.5	8.3	0.00149
20	−12.3	6.76	0.00126
25	−30.1	5.45	0.001066
30	−47.9	4.36	0.000888
35	−67.8	3.46	0.000737
40	−67.0	2.72	0.000581
45	−67.0	2.20	0.000469
50	−67.0	1.69	0.000358

The Properties of Some
Common Liquids at 68°F

Liquid	Sp gr	$\mu \times 10^5$ lb-sec/ft²	σ, lb/ft
Alcohol	0.8	2.4	0.0015
Benzine	0.88	1.36	0.002
Gasoline	0.8	0.63	0.0017
Glycerine	1.3	1,800	0.0043
Linseed oil	0.95	90	0.0023
Mercury	13.55	3.24	0.035
Olive oil	0.9	175	0.0023
Turpentine	0.85	3.11	0.0018
Water, fresh	1.0	2.09	0.005
Water, sea	1.03	3.2	0.006

The Properties of Some Common Gases at 68°F and Atmospheric Pressure

Gas	$\rho,$ slug/ft^3	$\mu \times 10^5$ lb-sec/ft^2	$R,$ ft/°R	k
Air	0.00238	0.0378	53.3	1.4
Carbon dioxide	0.00363	0.0305	34.9	1.28
Hydrogen	0.000166	0.0184	767	1.4
Nitrogen	0.00229	0.0363	55.1	1.4
Oxygen	0.00262	0.0417	48.3	1.4

A List of Important Equations

Application	*Equation*
Shear stress–viscosity relationship	$\tau = \mu \dfrac{dv}{dy}$
Excess pressure within a soap bubble	$p = \dfrac{4\sigma}{d}$
Pressure-density-height relationship	$p = \gamma h$
Large-ended U-tube manometer	$p = y\left[\gamma_1\left(1 + \dfrac{a}{A}\right) - \gamma_2\left(1 - \dfrac{a}{A}\right)\right]$
Depth of the center of pressure below centroid	$x = \dfrac{I_0}{Ah_c}$
Pressure in a vertically accelerated fluid	$p = h\gamma\dfrac{a + g}{g}$
Surface angle of a horizontally accelerated fluid	$\tan\theta = \dfrac{a}{g}$
Surface profile of a radially accelerated fluid	$y = \dfrac{\omega^2 r^2}{2g}$
Equation of continuity	$\rho A V = \text{const}$
Euler's equation	$0 = \dfrac{dp}{\gamma} + \dfrac{v\,dv}{g} + dz$
Bernoulli's equation for incompressible flow	$\dfrac{p}{\gamma} + \dfrac{V^2}{2g} + z = \text{const}$
Torricelli's equation	$V = \sqrt{2gh}$

Application	*Equation*

Aerodynamic form of Bernoulli's equation

$$p + \tfrac{1}{2}\rho V^2 = \text{const}$$

Flow rate through a venturi meter

$$Q = C_v A_2 \sqrt{\frac{2g(p_1/\gamma + z_1 - p_2/\gamma - z_2)}{1 - (A_2/A_1)^2}}$$

Flow rate through an orifice meter

$$Q = C_v C_o A_2 \sqrt{\frac{2g(p_1/\gamma + z_1 - p_2/\gamma - z_2)}{1 - C_o^2(A_2/A_1)^2}}$$

Free vortex flow

$$vr = \text{const}$$

Liquid compressibility

$$K = -\frac{\Delta p}{\Delta V/V}$$

Universal gas law

$$\frac{p}{\gamma} = RT$$

Adiabatic gas law

$$\frac{p}{\gamma^k} = \text{const}$$

Velocity of sound

$$c = \sqrt{kgRT}$$

Bernoulli's equation for compressible flow in its various forms

$$\frac{V_2^2 - V_1^2}{2g} = \frac{p_2 k}{\gamma_2(k-1)}\left[\left(\frac{\gamma_1}{\gamma_2}\right)^{k-1} - 1\right]$$

$$= \frac{p_2 k}{\gamma_2(k-1)}\left[\left(\frac{p_1}{p_2}\right)^{(k-1)/k} - 1\right]$$

$$= \frac{Rk}{k-1}(T_1 - T_2)$$

The stagnation pressure in compressible flow

$$p_s = p_0 + \tfrac{1}{2}\rho_0 V_0^2\left(1 + \frac{M^2}{4} + \cdots\right)$$

Mach number behind a normal shock wave

$$M_2 = \left\{\frac{1 + [(k-1)/2]M_1^2}{kM_1^2 - (k-1)/2}\right\}^{1/2}$$

Pressure ratio across a normal shock wave

$$\frac{p_2}{p_1} = \frac{1 + kM_1^2}{1 + kM_2^2}$$

Temperature ratio across a normal shock wave

$$\frac{T_2}{T_1} = \frac{1 + [(k-1)/2]M_1^2}{1 + [(k-1)/2]M_2^2}$$

Critical pressure ratio

$$\left(\frac{p_2}{p_1}\right)_{\text{crit}} = \left(\frac{2}{k+1}\right)^{k/(k-1)}$$

Impulse-momentum equation

$$\mathbf{F} = Q\rho(\mathbf{V}_2 - \mathbf{V}_1)$$

Torque–angular-momentum equation

$$T = Q\rho(r_1 V_{t_1} - r_2 V_{t_2})$$

Flow velocity through an ideal propeller

$$V = \frac{V_4 + V_1}{2}$$

Application	*Equation*
Propeller efficiency	$\eta = \dfrac{V_1}{V}$
Reynolds number	$N_R = \dfrac{VL}{\nu}$
Froude number	$N_F = \dfrac{V^2}{gL}$
Force on an immersed moving object	$F = C_F \tfrac{1}{2}\rho V^2 L^2$
Head loss in laminar flow between flat parallel stationary plates	$h_L = \dfrac{12\mu VL}{\gamma t^2}$
Head loss in laminar flow in circular pipes	$h_L = \dfrac{32\mu VL}{\gamma D^2}$
Blasius seventh root law	$v = 1.24V\left(\dfrac{y}{a}\right)^{\frac{1}{7}}$
Darcy-Weisbach equation	$h = f\dfrac{L}{D}\dfrac{V^2}{2g}$
Loss due to pipe obstructions	$h = k\dfrac{V^2}{2g}$
Chézy-Manning equation	$V = \dfrac{1.5}{n}R^{\frac{1}{6}}\sqrt{RS}$
Critical depth	$y_c = \sqrt[3]{\dfrac{q^2}{g}}$
	$\quad = \tfrac{2}{3}E_{min}$
Aircraft lift	$L = C_L \tfrac{1}{2}\rho V^2 S$
Drag	$D = C_D \tfrac{1}{2}\rho V^2 S$
Drag coefficient	$C_D = C_{D_z} + C_{D_i}$
Aspect ratio	$A = \dfrac{2s}{\bar{c}} = \dfrac{S}{\bar{c}^2}$
Drag coefficient	$C_D = C_{D_z} + \dfrac{k}{\pi A}C_L^2$
Minimum drag	$D_{min} = 2W\sqrt{\dfrac{kC_{D_z}}{\pi A}}$
Minimum drag speed	$V_{md} = \sqrt[4]{\dfrac{4kW^2}{\pi A C_{D_z}\rho^2 S^2}}$

Application	*Equation*
Best gliding angle	$\dfrac{L}{D} = \cot\theta$
Climbing thrust	$\dfrac{T_c}{T} = \cos\theta\left(1 + \dfrac{L}{D}\tan\theta\right)$
Climbing power	$\dfrac{H_c}{H} = \cos^{3/2}\theta\left(1 + \dfrac{L}{D}\tan\theta\right)$
Banked turn	$\tan\phi = \dfrac{V^2}{gR}$
	$\sec\phi = \dfrac{L}{W}$
Pitching moment	$M = C_m\tfrac{1}{2}\rho V^2 S\bar{c}$
Stability condition	$\dfrac{dC_m}{d\alpha} < 0$
Tail volume ratio	$\bar{V} = \dfrac{S_T l_T}{S\bar{c}}$
Static margin:	
Stick fixed	$-h_n = \dfrac{h}{\bar{c}} - \bar{V}\dfrac{a_1}{a}\left(1 - \dfrac{d\epsilon}{d\alpha}\right)$
Stick free	$-h'_n = \dfrac{h}{\bar{c}} - \bar{V}\dfrac{a_1}{a}\left(1 - \dfrac{d\epsilon}{d\alpha}\right)\left(1 - \dfrac{a_2 b_1}{a_1 b_2}\right)$

Selected References

Albertson, M. R., J. R. Barton, and D. B. Simons: "Fluid Mechanics for Engineers," Prentice-Hall, Inc., Englewood Cliffs, N.J., 1960.

Bakhmeteff, B. A.: "Hydraulics of Open Channels," McGraw-Hill Book Company, Inc., New York, 1932.

Binder, R. C.: "Fluid Mechanics," Prentice-Hall, Inc., Englewood Cliffs, N.J., 1959.

Brenkert, Karl: "Elementary Theoretical Fluid Mechanics," John Wiley & Sons, Inc., New York, 1960.

Dwinnell, James H.: "Principles of Aerodynamics," McGraw-Hill Book Company, Inc., New York, 1949.

Francis, J. R. D.: "A Text-book of Fluid Mechanics," Edward Arnold (Publishers) Ltd., London, 1958.

Lewitt, E. H.: "Hydraulics and Fluid Mechanics," Sir Isaac Pitman & Sons, Ltd., London, 1958.

Middlemiss, R. R.: "Differential and Integral Calculus," McGraw-Hill Book Company, Inc., New York, 1946.

Rouse, H., and J. W. Howe: "Basic Mechanics of Fluids," John Wiley & Sons, Inc., New York, 1956.

Streeter, V. L.: "Fluid Mechanics," McGraw-Hill Book Company, Inc., New York, 1958.

Vennard, J. K.: "Elementary Fluid Mechanics," John Wiley & Sons, Inc., New York, 1961.

Woodward, S. M., and C. J. Posey: "The Hydraulics of Steady Flow in Open Channels," John Wiley & Sons, Inc., New York, 1941.

Answers to Odd-numbered
Problems

1·1	1.3; −10.5; −8.0; −4.2 psig	2·27	450 ft³
		2·29	8.05 ft/sec²
1·3	458 tons	2·31	36 ft³; 0; 338 lb
1·5	14.1 lb; 0.281 in.	2·33	736; 440 lb
1·7	1.304 lb	2·35	0.802 psig
1·9	0.0012 lb	3·1	15.3 fps
1·11	0.022 lb	3·3	24.9 psia
1·13	0.00868 lb-sec/ft²	3·5	1.63
1·15	0.305 in. below	3·7	0.506 cfs
2·1	88.9 psig. 211.5 in. Hg	3·9	10.05 cfs
2·3	14.8 psia	3·11	163 hp
2·5	3.21 psi	3·13	1.59 hp
2·7	13.05 psi	3·15	139 psf
2·9	11.8 ft	3·17	41.7; 167; 376 lb
2·11	306 in.	3·19	5.5 cfs
2·13	6.34 in.	3·21	0.108; 0.107 cfs
2·15	24,000 lb; 5.33 ft deep	3·23	317 mph
2·17	1.82×10^8 lb; 8.0° from the vertical, passing through the base 0.34 ft left of center	3·25	9.7 in.
		4·1	300,000 psi
		4·3	2780°F
2·19	6 ft	4·5	0.521 lb/ft³
2·21	25.5×10^6 lb	4·7	−62°F
2·23	15,700 lb	4·9	485°F; 117.6 psia; 0.336 lb/ft³
2·25	3.9 ft		

4·11 1,120; 865 fps
4·13 21.6 lb/sec; 7°F; 0.98
4·15 2.14
4·17 5.96 psia
4·19 14.7 psia
4·23 27.8 psia; 0.5 lb/sec
4·25 2.21 in.
5·1 104 lb downstream
5·3 2.04 lb
5·5 137.5 lb
5·7 156 fps; 0.305 in.
5·9 0.55 hp
5·11 103 rpm; 24,500 ft-lb; 480 hp
5·13 8.8 hp; 7.7 psi
5·15 662 lb
5·17 190 mph
5·19 4,150 lb; 166 hp
6·7 1,000 lb
6·9 8.4
6·11 $\frac{1}{6}$; $0.408V$
7·1 126; 4.94×10^{-4} lb-sec/ft^2
7·3 14.5 psig; 147
7·5 1,755; 5.05×10^{-4} ft^2/sec

7·7 100 psi
7·9 0.34 cfs
8.1 0.0468
8·3 1.82 ft
8·5 2 ft
8·7 Rapid; 22.1 fps; 25.1; 22.7 ft-lb/lb
8·9 2 ft; 16.1 cfs/ft
8·11 3 ft
9·1 204; 236; 278; 330 fps; 3,910 lb; 162; 188; 221; 264 fps; 201; 233; 274; 327 fps; 4.5°
9·3 453; 448; 435; 396 fps; 2,880; 1,920; 1,100; 260 fpm; 225; 250; 290; 300 fps
9·5 12°; 224 fps; 5,900 lb
10·1 0.75; $0.078\bar{c}$; $0.101\bar{c}$; 7.4; 9.7 in.; $0.578\bar{c}$; $0.601\bar{c}$ (behind leading edge); yes; stick free
10·3 2.12; 2.31 ft; improved
10·5 7.8°; −1.3°

Index